THE
HUMBLE
ESSAY

SECOND EDITION

THE
HUMBLE
ESSAY

SECOND EDITION

Roy K. Humble

Problem Child Press

Dallas, Oregon

Contents

Introduction

Learning to Write

Even in this deluxe second edition, *The Humble Essay* still lacks almost everything you're likely to find in a respectable composition textbook. It lacks attractive graphics, plastic tabs, questions for discussion, and an index. It offers no bonus DVD, no laminated cheat sheet, no interactive website. You might wonder why this book lacks so many of the usual ingredients. The answer is simple — you don't need all that stuff.

To learn how write an effective college essay, you only need a few ingredients. One is a set of sensible guidelines, which is what you'll find in *The Humble Essay* — in language you can understand without becoming an English major. If this little book has one thing going for it, that's it. It's also a good idea to work with someone who is better at writing than you are, someone who can help you apply these guidelines and check your progress. A writing professor comes to mind.

The most important requirement, however, is simply that you write, and write a lot, so you can see for yourself what it means to put these guidelines into practice. Learning to write the college essay is like learning how to French kiss. Reading about it will only take you so far. To really learn how to do it, you have to actually do it — again and again and again.

If you're reading this book because it's part of a class you're taking, you should pause now and give quiet thanks for all the writing assignments that will soon be coming your way. They, more than anything, will help you put these guidelines into practice. Embrace these assignments with gusto and the blind faith that they will do you some good. If you're going to learn anything of lasting value in a writing class, your assignments will teach it to you.

Don't be afraid of struggling, either. You're learning new skills here, and making mistakes will be an important part of the process. So make your mistakes, correct them, and then move on to more sophisticated errors. It's not a big deal.

When I was in first grade, I once came home yelling for my mother because I'd gotten a frowny face on a math test. My class had moved into subtraction without any warning, and I'd missed seven out of ten problems. Mom was out delivering some fine Amway products to her customers, but my sister Nadine was in the living room practicing for her interpretive dance recital. I told her about the shameful frowny face.

"It's just math," she said, waving her arms to simulate a tree enlivened by a summer breeze. "*Anyone* can learn math."

That was one of the kindest things my sister ever said to me. It gave me the courage to return to school the next day and begin the hard work of learning how to subtract.

It's the same with the college essay. It might *feel* overwhelming at first, but it's just writing. It's just the college essay. You don't need fancy books or cumbersome websites or DVDs. You just need to keep writing. *Anyone* can learn how to do this, and that includes you.

CHAPTER 1

THE COLLEGE ESSAY IS YOUR IDEA

The college essay is defined by what it does, and it only does one thing. It explains one idea of your own — your opinion, in other words.

The word "opinion" is often used as a synonym for "guess" or "hunch," an idea that you think *might* be true even if you have little or no reason to think so. That's not the sort of opinion we're talking about here. For a college essay, the main idea must be a *reasonable* opinion, an idea that's based on thoughtful consideration of your topic. As long as what you write presents your reasonable opinion, it's an essay.

I wish it were more complicated so I could explain it to you more impressively, but it really is that simple. Or it would be that simple if so many of your teachers hadn't confused the issue by playing fast and loose with the word "essay."

Since grade school, you've heard this word used to describe just about anything made with sentences. Your high school English teachers haven't helped matters by tossing around technical terms as if you understood them — or cared. So before we move on to the important work of learning how to write the college essay, we'll start by clearing up some common misunderstandings.

COMMONLY MISUNDERSTOOD TERMS

It's beyond the scope of this little book to clean up *all* the misunderstandings that you've received from your teachers over the years, but we do need to untangle four important terms that will be used to explain how essays work: thesis, thesis statement, topic, and topic sentence. This won't take too long, but you will need to care just a little about the correct definitions so that the chapters that follow will make more sense to you.

THESIS AND THESIS STATEMENT

The word "thesis" is a Greek term that means "proposal" or "assertion." When talking about college essays, thesis means "your main idea." English teachers like to use "thesis" in place of "main idea" because it's a Greek word, and there's something about Greek words that make English teachers purr with contentment. I don't understand why, either. That's just how it is.

As long as you understand that "thesis" means "main idea," Greek-loving English teachers won't pose a serious problem for you. However, keep in mind that the thesis of an essay is not the same as the "thesis statement." The thesis is your idea, a bit of electrochemical activity inside your brain. The thesis statement is a written sentence that *states* your *thesis*. See how that works? It translates the intangible idea that lives in your brain into tangible words on an actual piece of paper or computer screen.

Here's a table, for those who like tables:

THESIS AND THESIS STATEMENT

	Thesis	Thesis Statement
Definition	An assertion, the main idea of an essay	A written sentence that articulates a thesis into actual words
Key Quality	Exists only as an idea — intangible	Exists only as written words, a sentence — tangible

The distinction between "thesis" and "thesis statement" seems easy enough to keep in mind, but there are a few rogue English teachers who confuse this as well by using "thesis" for both your main idea and the written sentence that defines your main idea. When you run into these teachers, you have to pay attention to how they use "thesis" in a sentence. If they ask you *what* your thesis is, they are really saying, "What is your main idea?" If they ask *where* your thesis is, they are really saying, "Where in your essay have you hidden a one-sentence summary of your main idea? Because I'll be honest with you, student writer, I can't find it. Not anywhere."

For an essay to really be an essay, by the way, it needs to have a thesis, not a thesis statement. There's nothing wrong with putting a thesis statement in your essay. It tells your readers what your thesis is, and that's a good thing. But by itself, a thesis statement doesn't turn your paper into an essay. To write an essay, all of those sentences and paragraphs must collectively explain and defend an actual thesis. The opening must introduce that main idea. The body must explain that idea in detail. The closing must emphasize that same main idea one last time. That's what it means to have a thesis, and that's what it means to write an essay.

THESIS AND TOPIC

Some student writers have developed the habit of using "topic" and "thesis" interchangeably. This isn't surprising. "Topic" is a vague term, just like "thesis," and the term "topic sentence" refers to a sentence that states the main idea of a paragraph — the same thing that a thesis statement does for a whole essay. The similarity between "topic sentence" and "thesis statement" makes "topic" seem a lot like "thesis."

However, "topic" and "thesis" don't mean the same thing. The topic is the subject of the essay, the thing about which you have an idea — a story, a scientific theory, some horrible thing that happened to you, a historical figure, a movie, a political theory — *anything*. The thesis of an essay is your own informed opinion about that topic.

Perhaps this table will help:

TOPIC, THESIS, AND THESIS STATEMENT

	Topic	Thesis	Thesis Statement
Definition	The subject of an essay	The main idea of an essay	A written sentence that articulates the thesis
Example	Deer	The idea about deer that is explained by my essay	Deer are dangerous animals.
Example	Voting requirements	The idea about voting requirements that is explained by my essay	Voters should have to accurately describe what they're voting for before they can vote.
Example	The ending of "A Good Man is Hard to Find," by Flannery O'Connor	The idea I have about the ending that is explained by my essay	The ending of O'Connor's story teaches us how unsafe it is to reach out and touch someone.

For your essay to really be an essay, it must do more than discuss a topic or slip a thesis statement into the opening paragraph. The entire piece of writing must carefully introduce, explain, and defend your own reasonable idea about the topic.

TOPIC AND TOPIC SENTENCE

The last term to untangle is "topic sentence." You understand now that a topic is the subject that you study and about which you develop your own reasonable opinion. You might thus think that a topic sentence has something to do with the topic of your essay. That's a reasonable conclusion, logical student writer, but it's also completely wrong.

A topic sentence is instead a sentence that explains the purpose of a single paragraph within a longer piece of writing. The other sentences in the paragraph are called supporting sentences. They provide the more detailed information that actually accomplishes the purpose of that paragraph. Consider this paragraph and its topic sentence (in bold):

> **For an essay to really be an essay, by the way, it needs to have a thesis, not a thesis statement.** There's nothing wrong with putting a thesis statement in your essay. It tells your readers what your thesis is, and that's a good thing. But by itself, a thesis statement doesn't turn your paper into an essay. To write an essay, all of those sentences and paragraphs must collectively explain and defend an actual thesis. The opening must introduce that main idea. The body must explain that idea in detail. The closing must emphasize that same main idea one last time. That's what it means to have a thesis, and that's what it means to write an essay.

Supporting Paragraph

The topic sentence for this paragraph tells you the idea that this paragraph will explain — that an essay requires a thesis, not a thesis statement. The next two sentences explain that a thesis statement doesn't, by itself, turn something into an essay. The rest of the sentences then explain how a thesis must be present throughout a piece of writing for that piece of writing to be an essay. If you put together all of the supporting sentences, they explain the idea that's introduced by the topic sentence.

Sometimes a topic sentence states an idea that a paragraph explains. Sometimes it summarizes the information that a paragraph presents. Sometimes it tells us that a paragraph is an example of a larger idea. In all these cases, however, it has the same job to do. It tells us the purpose of that particular paragraph.

You probably don't need a table, but here's one anyway:

TOPIC, TOPIC SENTENCE, AND SUPPORTING SENTENCES

	Topic	Topic Sentence	Supporting Sentences
Definition	The subject of an essay (or in this case, a paragraph)	A written sentence that states the main purpose of a single paragraph	The sentences in a paragraph that illustrate or explain the idea stated by the topic sentence
Example	What makes an essay an essay	"For an essay to really be an essay, by the way, it needs to have a thesis, not a thesis statement."	"There's nothing wrong with putting a thesis statement into your essay.... That's what it means to write an essay."

THE COLLEGE ESSAY AND WHAT IT IS NOT

The most misunderstood term we have to consider is "essay." According to your teachers, you've been writing "essays" since the first day of third grade when beloved Mrs. Webster asked you to write an essay about your summer vacation. Since then, you've written hundreds of "essays" that were really stories, reports, reflection papers, and other types of writing — but not essays. To undo those long years of misunderstanding, we'll look at some of the non-essays from your past and compare them to the college essay. With each example, notice how the difference always comes back to whether or not its purpose is to present your own main idea.

COLLEGE ESSAYS AND STORIES

A story recounts events, real or imagined. Stories are usually organized chronologically, and they tend to focus on the actions of their characters. Stories engage readers because we're all suckers for finding out what happens next. For storytelling to be effective within an essay, however, you can't just present the series of events. You must use those events to explain a main idea. If you don't have a main idea to explain, then the story remains just a story. Here's an example of that:

> On the first night of our backpacking trip, Denise and I camped beside the river we'd followed upstream. We set up our tent on a small, sandy gravel bar to take advantage of the

Story

smooth ground and the soothing sound of the river. It was a beautiful campsite.

By the time we'd eaten, it was already getting dark, so Denise said we should leave the dishes for the morning. We took a few minutes to watch the stars come out, and then we hit the sack. Denise was asleep instantly.

It took me longer to fall asleep. Something didn't feel right. After perhaps an hour, I went outside to relieve myself. The stars had disappeared, but I didn't think anything of it. I went back to bed and finally fell asleep. Later that night, I woke to the sound of light rain on the tent. Like the river, it was a peaceful sound, and it lulled me back to sleep. The next time I woke, it was from Denise jabbing me with her elbow.

"Wake up!" she shouted. "We're soaked!"

We were more than soaked. It was raining heavily. The rising river had swamped our tent, washed our cooking gear downstream, and drenched our food. Scrambling in the pre-dawn darkness, we were lucky to get our tent, packs, and sleeping bags up to higher ground. We found most of the cooking gear later that day, but the food — and the trip — were ruined.

In this example, the story might be used to illustrate several ideas, but the author never explains one. Because no main idea is presented or even implied, the story remains just a story. Here's an example of how the writer could use this same experience to illustrate the main idea of an essay:

Whenever you go backpacking, the first rule is to respect the place you're traveling through. If you don't know this rule at the beginning of your backpack trip, the place itself will be glad to teach it to you. That's what happened to my former girlfriend and me last summer. It was our first backpacking trip together, and, perhaps because she wanted to impress me, Denise acted as if she were in control of everything — including the weather and the river.

On our first night out, I wanted to set up camp about thirty feet back from the river so we wouldn't have to worry about rising water during the night. Denise laughed at my suggestion and set up our tent at the water's edge. She left our cooking gear and food on the gravel beside the tent.

That night, however, it rained. It only rained lightly at our campsite, but upstream it rained heavily, and the river rose almost four inches before we woke. By then, our cooking gear was a hundred yards downstream and our food was soaked. Denise tried to laugh as if it was no big deal, but the fact is we could have been drowned in our sleep. And even though we escaped death, it took most of the day to recover the gear and dry things out.

This was a disappointing trip, but it taught me a lesson that has guided me ever since: Respect the environment or the environment will make you respect it. This is true when camping beside the river, but it's also true at home, at school, or driving down the street where you live. You should never assume you're in control of the world around you.

The writer uses the same story in this second example, but now he does more than just present the event. He uses the story to illustrate and validate his idea that one must respect one's surroundings. The main idea is now the star of the show, and the story has shifted to a supporting role. Because of this shift in purpose, we have an essay instead of a story.

Here's a table, in case you were expecting one:

COLLEGE ESSAY VS. STORY

	Story	Essay
Topic	A backpacking mishap	Having respect for the environment
Main Idea (as a thesis statement)	None	You should respect the environment you are in.
Explanation	The details of the story help readers understand the topic (a mishap) rather than an idea about the topic.	The details of the story explain why this piece of advice is a reasonable idea.

Autobiography is one type of storytelling that sometimes looks like an essay but still isn't. With autobiography, the author writes about the author: My life has always been difficult. Moving to Toledo is the best thing that ever happened to me. I sure like to watch sunsets. And so on. If the author presents one main idea about himself or herself, then technically it *is* an essay. However, it's not much of an essay because the topic (me!) isn't relevant to most college classes. Most college classes focus on something other than the students who take them.

Even so, autobiography can still be used effectively in an essay. Personal experiences draw readers into an essay, particularly if you come across as likable, someone the readers can relate to, and if the personal experience is relevant to your main idea. You just need to keep the autobiography in a supporting and appropriate role.

COLLEGE ESSAYS AND REPORTS

Reports give readers information about a topic. They are common in elementary and high school, and they persist as college assignments, too. A report is a good assignment because it requires students to inform themselves about a topic, and that's a valuable skill. Reports aren't essays, however, because they don't offer the author's own opinion about a topic.

In fact, it's fairly easy to write a perfectly acceptable report without thinking at all, as you probably know from experience. Think of the times when you simply opened a book and copied down the information "in your own words" without letting any of it penetrate your brain. Think of the times when you scoured the Internet for the first website that had any information on your topic. Here's a typical report:

> Pigdogs live in packs of six to eight animals in established territories of up to one square mile. The territory tends to be bounded by natural features, such as rivers, or by man-made features, such as interstate highways or fences. The territory includes a year-round source of water and a shaded area known as the "sty" where the pigdogs lounge as often as they are able and occasionally yip in their sleep.
>
> Females bear one litter of seven or eight pigpups every other year, except in times of drought. During times of drought, the females typically band together and fight off any rutting males, sometimes ferociously.
>
> The males are the hunters of the pack, although they will retreat from any animal that moves quickly, such as a rabbit or vole. Often they come back to the pack bearing fast-food wrappers and Pepsi cups or road kill that is not too intimidat-

Report

ing. They may also stalk fruit and vegetables, acting as if the plants were dangerous animals, and bring these spoils back to the sty with great displays of pride.

In this example, the author provides information that informs you about the topic of pigdogs. That makes it a report. For it to become an essay, the author needs to present his or her own idea about the topic and then use information about pigdogs to explain that idea.

Here's an example of an essay that uses the information about pigdogs to defend the author's opinion:

Non-native species have a way of destroying the environments they invade, and that's why the California Department of Fish and Wildlife must act more aggressively in its attempts to eradicate these species. A good illustration of failed eradication can be found in the case of the Norwegian pigdogs that have taken over large parts of California's Central Valley.

Pigdogs run in packs of five to eight animals over small territories (often defined by roads or irrigation ditches). They first arrived in California as pets on a Norwegian freighter, the *Ibsen*, which docked in Sacramento in 1911. Having been thrown overboard by the sailors, the pigdogs swam to shore and soon flourished in the surrounding environment.

Perhaps because they seem timid, or because of their odd habit of gathering roadside garbage, pigdogs have been considered harmless for decades. It was only recently that wildlife biologists observed that pigdogs had begun to crowd out native species such as raccoons. Efforts to curb the spread of pigdogs by removing roadside garbage only resulted in pigdogs moving into farmers' fields and orchards where they began a population explosion that continues today.

> If more aggressive eradication tactics — trapping, shoot-ing, poisoning — had been taken earlier, pigdogs would not now be eating one-third of California's annual artichoke crop, among other things.

This writer uses much of the same information about pig-dogs, but it's now used to present and defend an opinion. Any of the original information that didn't help to support that opinion has been dropped in the second example because the essay didn't need it. Here's another table, just in case:

COLLEGE ESSAY VS. REPORT

	Report	*Essay*
Topic	Pigdogs	Eradicating non-native species from California
Main Idea (as a thesis statement)	None	The California Depart-ment of Fish and Wild-life must act more ag-gressively to eradicate non-native species.
Explanation	Specific information helps readers better understand the topic of pigdogs.	The negative example of pigdog proliferation defends the idea that aggressive measures should be taken.

Paraphrasing is a type of report that looks a lot like an essay. With paraphrasing, the author reports *someone else's* opinion by putting that idea into his or her own words. While the presence of an opinion makes the piece of writing *look* like an essay, it remains a report because the main idea is not an idea that came from the author's own brain. Here's an example:

> When students complain that teachers have screamed profanities in the classroom, many parents' first response is often to file a complaint. However, according to *Detached Educator*, the newsletter of the Almost Retired Teachers Association (ARTA), that might not be the best approach.
>
> "An incident of screaming can admittedly cause temporary problems," says Richard Stevens, ARTA president, "but why make things worse by making a big deal about it?" According to Stevens, it's best to let the situation resolve itself over the course of several months, or even years.

You will regularly need to paraphrase the ideas of others. It's a good way to compress and include their ideas as you explain your own main idea. It just can't be a substitute for your own thinking.

COLLEGE ESSAYS AND REFLECTION PAPERS

A reflection paper is a collection of opinions or observations that are united only by their relevance to a given topic. The assignment is usually open-ended — explain your reactions to Chapter 3, describe what you find most interesting about this article, and so on. Teachers often assign reflection papers to compel you to do the reading that's been assigned. Why you wouldn't do the reading on your own is a mystery to your professors, but they embrace that mystery by assigning these free-form papers. Even if you're not willing to make the most of your tuition dollars, they're willing to force the issue. However, even if a reflection paper is assigned by a college professor, it isn't a college essay because it doesn't focus on one main idea.

Out in the real world, you sometimes find reflection papers in the letters-to-the-editor section of the local newspaper. Someone gets steamed about the way teachers have summers off, or how baseball players shouldn't wear baggy pants — or whatever else — and they respond to the situation by typing rapidly. What comes out of their fingertips *seems* coherent because it sticks to one topic and is unified by the same angry mood, but unless what's written sticks to one main idea, it is not, as you might have guessed, an essay.

Within the academic world, an essay assignment can easily turn into a reflection paper if writers either can't decide what to say or are unwilling to take a single position. Instead, they write circles around a topic and hope that it will miraculously become an essay. Occasionally this kind of rambling does generate a miracle, but don't be encouraged by that.

Here's an example of a typical reflection paper on the venerable topic of "writing":

> Writing is important. You have to be able to write in order to succeed in our society. People expect you to write well. If you can't express yourself well as a writer, then you will miss out on many important opportunities.
>
> The use of writing has been with us for thousands of years, but in the past only the elite needed to write. Since the invention of the printing press, however, writing has become more important with each passing year, until now almost

everyone needs to write. Nowadays, with the arrival of computers and email and texting, writing is even more essential to the world in which we live.

It isn't easy to learn to be a good writer, but a good teacher can help you to gain the skills that will make you a better writer. You will find that with stronger skills, you have much more confidence, and confidence translates into success!

Oy vey.

If you're assigned to write a reflection paper about a topic, then reflect all you want with as many ideas as you want. However, if you're assigned to write an essay, you need to make sure it doesn't turn into a reflection paper.

One way to prevent that from happening is to resist the urge to simply vent your emotions. An essay is not a yelling match with your boyfriend about how he doesn't provide the emotional support you need and how he has, in this and fifteen other ways, failed to meet your expectations. Emotions are fine, but they aren't the same as thinking.

Second, you must take some time to actually figure out what you think about a topic. Do that *before* you start writing your essay. Don't start gushing words onto the page about a topic and hope that somehow an idea will emerge or that, in the absence of an idea, your professor will be impressed by your use of many fine, long words. With your friends, you might call that sort of writing "B.S." Your professors have other and worse names for it.

Here is how a writer might start to turn one of the rambling ideas from that last example into an essay:

In a recent *People* magazine poll, 59 percent of the respondents said that writing freaked them out. On a recent television reality show, only one of six participants was willing to write a typical college-level essay, even when offered a hundred dollars. The problem? People feel inadequate about their writing skills. But that all seems to be changing, thanks to the Internet. To use the Internet you have to read and you have to write.

Most of that reading and writing happens when Internet users send, receive, and respond to email. Chat rooms require less formal writing but they require more of it and at a faster pace. Using the websites as a source of information doesn't require the same level of writing, but social networking sites such as Facebook use writing extensively.

Even though many users may not be aware of how much writing they are doing, the writing still has its impact. Internet users, whether they realize it or not, are becoming more and more comfortable with the written word.

According to Dr. Jay Trabue of Northern Central University, it all comes down to classical conditioning. Writing within a more comfortable environment helps writers to associate that feeling of comfort with the writing itself. And that makes them feel more adequate as writers. He notes that while 59 percent of *People* magazine readers are still freaked out about writing, that number is down from 63 percent two years ago.

So while the growing use of the Internet makes writing more important, that growing importance does not seem to be making people more uncomfortable with writing. Instead, it seems to be helping them become more confident and prolific writers.

In this version, the writer stays focused on just one reasonable opinion about writing, and each paragraph has a clear connection to that thesis. The opening paragraph introduces the topic and the main idea about that topic. The next paragraph illustrates how much writing is involved in using the Internet. Then there is a transition, and the next paragraphs explain how all that writing may change how people feel about their writing skills. The last paragraph summarizes the explanation provided by the body of the essay and, in doing so, again emphasizes the main idea.

Here is another table that may or may not help:

COLLEGE ESSAY VS. REFLECTION PAPER

	Reflection Paper	*Essay*
Topic	The importance of writing	Impact of increased Internet use on attitudes toward writing
Main Idea (as a thesis statement)	There is no main idea. Each paragraph contains one or more different ideas about the topic.	The increased use of the Internet seems to be making people more confident writers because it requires so much writing.
Explanation	Because the essay skips from idea to idea, no single idea is illustrated with more than a broad and passing summary of information.	Paragraph 2 illustrates the increased amounts of writing required. Paragraphs 3 and 4 explain *how* attitudes are changing among Internet users.

College Essays and Five-Paragraph Trainer-Essays

The "essay" you wrote in high school was almost certainly a five-paragraph trainer-essay. The trainer-essay is to a real essay what a training bra is to a real bra. It might make you feel like you're grown up enough to write a real essay, but it's almost never an actual, fully developed essay.

The five-paragraph trainer-essay is mostly just an organizational template. An introductory paragraph presents the topic and main idea. Each of three body paragraphs then covers one subtopic or idea about the main topic. A concluding paragraph restates the main idea and the point of each of the body paragraphs. Into this template you can insert anything you want as long as it's related to the main topic. If you insert raw information into the body paragraphs, it becomes a five-paragraph report. If you insert a new idea of into each of the body paragraphs, it becomes a five-paragraph reflection paper.

The five-paragraph trainer-essay is taught because it's easy for teachers to explain and easy for students to use. It's something a beginning writer can accomplish at an early age. The problem is that adherence to an organizational format like this tends to generate essays that oversimplify and under-explain your thinking. That might be fine when you're young and don't have anything to say anyway, but with the college essay, your main idea will always be more important than any kind of organizational template.

The format needs to fit the idea and not vice versa. If an idea can be explained in five paragraphs, then fine, write a five-paragraph essay. So be it. But if the idea is more complex and requires six or twelve or sixteen supporting paragraphs, then so be that. Set your five-paragraph trainer-essay aside and get on with the task of writing college essays.

COLLEGE ESSAYS AND GREAT ESSAYS

There are even better essays out there, of course. The college essay introduced in this book is just a start. It gets the job done, and it does so simply and effectively. But while it's better than what you wrote in high school, it's still not a *great* essay.

Great essays, like the ones you might find in respected magazines and overpriced college anthologies, use more advanced methods to present their main ideas. The venerable E. B. White, for example, could write an essay about watching his son jump into a lake and, in sharing his simple observations, somehow unravel the mysteries of the life cycle. He did this with careful arrangement of images, with careful selection of words, and with only minor and understated discussion of his idea. If you didn't know any better, you might think it was a reflection paper or a story.

If you didn't know any better, you might also be tempted to skip over the sensible guidelines in this book and get right to the task of writing your own great essays. The thing about great essays, however, is that while they are easy to read, they are difficult to write. For most of us, they are out of reach while we're in college. Or while we're in grad school. Or while we're slogging through life teaching English composition for part-time wages at a community college in the middle of nowhere.

Another problem with great essays is that, aside from a few young and still-untarnished English professors, your college professors aren't particularly interested in reading them. They want to see your ideas about the topics they've assigned, and they want to see your ideas explained clearly and concisely. They have dozens of other papers to read besides yours, too, so they will become ill-tempered if you stray from your assigned task in order to unravel the mysteries implicit in your recent journey to the refrigerator.

Don't lose heart over this, potentially aspiring student writer. Greatness might indeed be part of your future. It's probably not, but it might be. In the meantime, though, you have college essays to write — essays that are due next Thursday, or possibly tomorrow morning — and for these assignments, you will do well with the basic essay introduced here.

I'm not saying that you shouldn't be creative and put some heart into your work. You should, for your own sake most of all. We'll talk more about that later. Just don't work too hard to dazzle a professor when all she or he really wants is a single good idea translated clearly into words. The rest of this book will explain how to do that.

CHAPTER 2

THE COLLEGE ESSAY

IS A LEARNING

PROCESS

Student writers often think of the college essay as a thing, something they have made, pages of paper with words on them. In one sense, they're right. The essay is a physical object that they produce. It's something that they hand to their professors and that their professors read, grade, and hand back.

The college essay does not create itself, however. It's the result of something that student writers do. And for the essay to be any good, the majority of work needs to happen before any typing takes place. So while it makes some sense to think of the essay as a product, it makes more sense to think of it as a process, a set of steps that help student writers to discover a good idea and then present that idea on paper.

For the college essay, the writing process usually has three main steps:

1. **Educate yourself about your topic.** This includes getting to know your topic generally and then digging deeper into the information about that topic to understand its complexities more clearly. This allows you to develop your own conclusions about what that information means.

2. **Identify and then improve one good idea of your own about the topic.** This means articulating your idea clearly in the words of a single sentence — the thesis statement — and then improving that idea by making the thesis statement more precise and accurate.

3. **Carefully present your idea.** This means planning your essay, drafting it, and then revising and proofreading it to make it as effective as possible.

The process can have a lot of variations. With argumentative writing, for example, the first step divides into two steps — first, identifying a debatable question about a topic, and second, educating yourself by examining relevant information. With scientific papers, you might start with a hypothesis and then test that idea by gathering more information about the topic. However, the same basic pattern persists. You begin in relative ignorance about a topic, then you work hard to enlighten yourself, and then you present one your enlightening ideas to others in an essay. Most of the work is not actually writing but educating yourself about your topic so that you'll have something worth writing about.

This chapter begins with a look at some common and misguided approaches to the writing process. We'll then look more closely at how you should follow the three steps of a more thoughtful process. You will thus be able to clean out any misconceptions and replace them with a more practical and effective method for writing your own college essays.

THINKING FOR YOURSELF

When I ask a new class of writing students to explain their process for writing essays, most of them respond with a strange combination of ignorance and confidence. For these writers, the writing process is essentially a mystery, but it's a mystery that they have conquered with various rituals. Here's one sample explanation:

> Whenever I have to write an essay, I sit in my room and turn off all the lights except for the computer monitor, which goes to a screen saver of traveling through the universe, like on *Star Trek*. I light a candle to help me relax. Vanilla is good. After that, I wait for an idea to come to me. Usually something comes to me within five minutes. I never question what it is. I just go with it. I write until I get it all out and onto paper — or the computer. Then I stop. If there's time, I come back later to check spelling and stuff, but I almost never change anything.

Good luck with not changing anything, student writer.

A second common method is just as magical, but it's less overtly so. This process relies on the subconscious mind:

> When I need to write an essay, the first thing I do is go to the library or Wikipedia and just read about it for like an

> hour. Sometimes I take longer, but only if I'm into it. Then I just write about whatever I've read. The information all kind of flows together onto the page. I go over it once to smooth things out, but if I spend more time than that, the process starts to break down.

The process starts to break down, semiconscious student writer, because it's not a process. You're relying on your subconscious mind to piece together whatever information is floating around in your brain. When you *consciously* examine what you've written, you see that you have no idea what you're doing.

A third common approach depends less on magic or the subconscious mind and more on other people. This isn't exactly plagiarism, but it does rely on something other than the student writer's ability to think. Here's an example:

> Whenever I have a paper assignment, my mother and I sit down and talk things through, and she lets me know when I have something that seems like it would be a good paper. Then I go off and write it on my own. That might take an hour. Then we work on revising it together. She was a teacher for many years, so she knows about how to write papers. She's the one who taught me that an essay should have three supporting paragraphs, which I still think is the best way to do it. None of my previous teachers have had any problems with it. In fact, I have always gotten excellent grades in all my English classes UNTIL THIS TERM. I used to enjoy writing — A LOT.

Sorry for ruining your life, student writer!

What you see in each of these three examples is an abdication of the writers' responsibility to think for themselves.

Instead, they let their moms or their subconscious minds or mysterious forces of the universe do the thinking for them. They seem to believe that the writing process is more powerful than the writer, and that they have no choice but to follow whatever process they've fallen into. However, writing the college essay is just a set of actions that can be learned and improved upon. No magic is required. Mothers are optional. This process might feel awkward at first, especially if you set aside something comfortable like vanilla-scented candles, but awkward is normal. When it comes to learning new things, awkward is a promising sign that you're getting somewhere.

The more you practice a new process, the more comfortable it becomes, until eventually you can look back at your former process and smile nostalgically at what a goofball you used to be. You've done this a hundred times before with a hundred other new skills. It's not like you left the womb knowing how to tie your shoes or drive a car or find a moderately priced Thai restaurant. Learning how to write a college essay might take some time, but it's still just something you do, a process you can learn to do on your own. And it's *nothing* compared to something really difficult like ballroom dancing.

At some dark moment in your past, a teacher might have told you that you were just a bad writer, as if bad writing was a rash, and you had it, and it wasn't going to get better. If you took that teacher's diagnosis seriously, you might be clinging desperately to whatever rituals seem to work. But here's the real story with an incident like that — your teacher was just a bad teacher. You might not have had the skills you needed to be an effective writer *at the time*, but your teacher was blaming you for his or her failure to teach you how to improve. What a rotten teacher! I'm sorry for your terrible luck.

Writing is neither a medical nor a genetic condition. People may naturally be more or less comfortable in their ability to use written language, just as they may naturally be more or less comfortable in their ability to remain upright on a skateboard. However, in the same way that anyone can learn how to use a skateboard, anyone can learn how to write a college essay. All you have to do is start out simply and get better with practice. You might not become a professional writer, but with enough practice, you *can* become competent and comfortable with a more thoughtful writing process.

Not Acting Like a Knucklehead

A fourth inadequate process is the most common of them all. It's the hardest to leave behind because it's worked so well for so many student writers. Here's one explanation:

> The way I write a paper is to figure out what I want to say and then look for info that will support it. I usually know what I want to say right away. Ideas just come to me like that. I'm not opinionated, but I have a lot of good ideas. If I can find enough stuff to support my idea, then I just start writing and put it all in the paper. If I can't find enough information, then either I start over with a different idea (hardly ever) or I use common knowledge to explain what I mean.

This explanation reminds me of waiting for my first swim lesson to begin, hanging out in the wading pool with all the other Pollywogs. I was intensely afraid of the big pool, so to convince my mother that I didn't need swim lessons, I laid down in the wading pool and used my arms to move around. "Mom!" I yelled. "Look! I can swim! I don't need lessons!" Mom barely looked up from her magazine. "That ain't swimming, Roy," she said. "That's just being a knucklehead." The other mothers laughed. I felt like an idiot, but Mom did have a point.

It's the same point I make to students when they use this particular process for writing the college essay. That ain't the college essay, student writer. That's just being a knucklehead. Yes, that thing you turned in *looks* like a college essay — you've got your own main idea and you've found information to back it up — but it's not a college essay because you've reversed the two central steps of the writing process.

The knucklehead writing process looks like this:

1. Decide on an idea. It's probably a hunch because you don't know much about your topic, but it might also be some idea you found quickly in a cursory look at the topic.
2. Examine the topic for information to back up that idea — and ignore any contradictory information or ideas.
3. Present the idea and the information that supports it.

This is the writing process of conspiracy theorists. They start with a suspicion: The mob assassinated President John

F. Kennedy. The September 11th attacks were an inside job. President Barack Obama wasn't born in America. Then they use that suspicion to judge whether information is credible or not. If a piece of information supports their suspicion, they say it's credible information. Anything that refutes their suspicion is just part of the conspiracy and is quickly rejected. Knuckleheads then use the information they accept to confirm that their suspicion is a good idea.

It's possible, of course, that a suspicion is also true. It's thus possible that a knucklehead's idea could become the main idea of a pretty good essay. However, that will only be an accidental outcome. Knuckleheads won't actually know whether their suspicions are good ideas or not because they won't have tested those ideas with an honest look at the information. Instead, they'll have tested the information with their suspicions. They haven't been open to other plausible, and possibly better, ideas. The idea they started with — good or bad — only becomes a more strongly held prejudice.

Thinking for yourself means being thoughtful about all of your ideas — no matter where they come from. It means educating yourself about a topic and then using that information to find the best available ideas. It means testing your ideas to make sure they're worthy of acceptance.

WRITING THE COLLEGE ESSAY

Learning how to write the college essay may not be a lot of fun at first. I hated swim lessons — and not just that first summer, either, but for the next two summers until I finally graduated from Pollywogs. It might be that kind of a struggle for you. Or you might be like my sister Nadine, who passed Pollywogs on her first attempt. You might have a strong aptitude for using words. You might have had a high school teacher who expected you to think for yourself and use information to form and test your ideas. Don't worry about how quickly you succeed with this process. The point is to push ahead, whether or not it comes easily, so that with practice you get better.

Here's how the college writing process breaks down into the three main steps that were mentioned at the start of this chapter. I'll use a hard-hitting local news story to illustrate how the process works.

STEP 1: EDUCATE YOURSELF ABOUT YOUR TOPIC

In college, the reason you're assigned essays is not so that you will write them. You're assigned essays so that you will have to deal first-hand with new topics and, in this way, educate yourself well enough about a topic that you can then write a thoughtful essay. The essay is just a byproduct of the more important self-education process that's required. That's why you so rarely get to write about yourself or topics you already understand and care about. Whether you intended it or not, you're paying your professors to give you *new* topics to under-stand and care about.

The first step toward a good essay, then, is to educate your-self about whatever topic is assigned to you, even if you hate it. This does not mean you have to fall in love with a topic. This has nothing to do with emotions. Understanding your topic is something you do, not something you feel.

The way to educate yourself about a topic is first of all to get to know it. You do that with general sources of information — reference books, textbooks, talking to your professor, visit-ing credible websites. As you become more educated about that topic, you will start to notice surprising or odd or challenging bits of information that spark your interest. You then narrow your focus to one of these more engaging points and dig deeper into the topic with more professional and scholarly sources of information that are more reliable and more detailed. Your closer examination of information will lead to your own con-clusions about what that information means, and one of those conclusions can then be used as the main idea of your essay.

Early in the term, I like to have students to read an article from the front page of a local newspaper and develop an essay in response. Suppose, for example, that an article explains how the city council has voted to impose a $50 tax on citizens who raise chickens within the city limits. Owners of chickens don't like the tax, but the city council says the tax is needed to pay for someone to oversee chicken raising operations, and that the only alternative would be to ban chickens entirely.

With a topic like this, you might start the writing process by getting to know the issue through the local newspaper. A newspaper is a general source of information that tries to cover all news items that are relevant to its readership. As such, it rarely gets into a lot of detailed information, but it does cover its topics, large or small, with at least a broad summary of all the important facts. That makes it a great resource for getting to know a local topic like this.

Something like a chicken tax doesn't make it onto a city council agenda without first generating complaints, so you can use the newspaper to find those complaints. They're probably in the letters-to-the-editor section as well as the news articles. What do the complainers have against chickens? How have the chicken owners responded? If you can't find anything more about chickens in your city newspaper, then look elsewhere. If chickens have been debated in your city, they've been debated in other cities. So you can look for editorials, articles, and letters to the editor in other cities' newspapers, too.

As you start out, you might have an opinion in mind about this topic. If so, don't be a knucklehead about it. Treat that opinion like the annoying cousin who's been sleeping on your couch for the last three weeks and shows no signs of leaving. Don't do anything to encourage it. You need to keep an open mind at this point, and that means setting aside any hunches about your topic. A hunch tends to limit your focus to information that's relevant to that idea, and you need to consider all the information you can find so that your idea will be as thoughtful as possible.

I'm serious about that, by the way. If there's one thing you need to learn about college writing, it's that it must be thoughtful. Hunches aren't thoughtful. Ready-made opinions aren't thoughtful. The ideas of your professor aren't (for you) thoughtful. The college essay is here to explain what *you* think, so you must think before you write it, and your thinking requires careful consideration of relevant information.

To dig a little deeper into the topic of raising chickens within city limits, you might read the actual transcript of the city council meeting to examine the information that was reported in the newspaper. Many cities put recordings of their meetings online now. You can listen to the full meeting. That would be fun. In some cases, experts might have already developed some fairly thoughtful conclusions about this topic. You can examine their ideas and reasoning and see how they hold up in your situation.

You might also talk to others who know more than you. With most college assignments, you can talk to your professor to get a better understanding of an issue and receive some guidance about where to look for information. This is particularly useful if you do some initial research and don't find much of anything. Reference librarians in your campus library are good resources, too. Or you may know someone whose job is related to your topic — your family doctor, your lawyer brother-in-law, the retired chicken inspector who moved into the apartment downstairs. Call your city councilor, who is a politician and therefore loves to talk. These local experts can all point you toward good, detailed, real-world information.

Once you start exploring a topic, you will be shocked and amazed to see the complexity of your topic expand outward in a dozen directions. That's why you need to narrow your focus to one smaller and engaging aspect of your topic. By narrowing your focus, you're able to invest more time in a smaller range of information. This allows you to become something of an expert on that subtopic, which is just the sort of preparation you need to be able to write about it.

Many student writers are skeptical of this kind of commitment to an assigned topic. They have more important things to do than educate themselves. Moreover, they have rarely had to do this in the past. To them, I say welcome to the rest of your life, unsuspecting student writer. The only thing you'll need to do from now until the grave is educate yourself about one new topic after another. It will often be a lot of fun, even when life assigns you all sorts of unexpected topics. And even when it's not any fun, the alternative — letting other people do your thinking for you — is far worse.

STEP 2: IDENTIFY AND IMPROVE YOUR MAIN IDEA

At some point, even with a topic as engaging and complex as chickens, you will run out of time for gathering and considering information about your topic. When that happens, you have to decide which of your ideas to write about. Your decision should be based on a few things — the assignment, your interest in the idea, and your honesty.

You need to show proper respect for the assignment by living within its boundaries. If you end up with an idea you love that's outside those boundaries, then at least talk to your instructor about getting a waiver to make sure your idea will be acceptable.

And as much as possible, try to keep yourself amused and engaged in the process by writing about an idea you like. If you take the time to educate yourself about your topic, you will have several to choose from. It's more rewarding to work with one of your own ideas than it is to write about some quick, knuckleheaded idea that you didn't discover yourself.

The honesty part comes from letting the information you find guide you toward the best ideas available. People usually narrow the focus of their writing to parts of a topic that are debatable or even controversial. With chickens, you might not be personally invested in an idea. That will make it easier for you to be honest about what the information tells you. However, if you're writing about something that matters to you, and if the information pulls you toward an idea you didn't expect and don't like, honesty can be a challenge. Be honest anyway. Don't be a knucklehead. Make sure that your idea is accurately founded on real-world information and reasonable thinking.

Your idea needs to be precise, too. Until you define your idea precisely, you've only *kind of* decided what you think. That's not good enough. A vague idea is just a hazy cluster of potential ideas and will often lead to a reflection paper rather than an essay. To define an idea precisely, you need to translate the idea into actual words and then tinker with those words until they define your idea exactly and accurately. Suppose, for example, that the information you find leads you to this conclusion:

> All chickens should be banned from within the city limits because they are noisy.

That seems reasonable enough to you. You found plenty of real-world information to confirm that chickens really are noisy. Roosters are the noisiest, but the incessant clucking of the hens can be just as irritating. So say the people who live near the chickens.

But it's not just the noise that bothers the neighbors. It's also the smell. Chickens, it turns out, have poor bathroom habits. This leads to what some would call an unpleasant aroma that hovers over the neighborhood like smog. That's a part of the idea, too, so you can make your idea more precise by including that fact in your reasoning:

> All chickens should be banned from within the city limits because they are noisy and because they stink up the entire neighborhood.

That's better. It relies on a broader range of information. However, now you remember the article you read about the people who own a breed of chickens that are mute and can be trained to relieve themselves in kitty litter. That information weakens your argument for banning chickens.

If you were still in high school, you would simply ignore the quiet, sweet-smelling breed of chicken and pretend your idea is invincible. Because you are in college, however, you decide to revise your idea so that it more honestly conforms to the more complex information you have gathered and considered:

> Chickens should be banned from within the city limits if they are noisy or if they stink up the neighborhood.

This is better. This sentence defines the boundaries of your idea more precisely. It's an idea you can more honestly defend, too, because it's a more honest idea. It will work well as the main idea of an essay. The idea still isn't perfect. It raises questions about implementation of that ordinance: What does it mean to be noisy? What does it mean to stink? Who will judge whether a flock of chickens is noisy or stinky? But that's a good sign, believe it or not. It means that you are moving into the complexities and complications of the real world. Good for you.

STEP 3: CAREFULLY PRESENT YOUR IDEA

Now, at last, it's time to share your thinking with others by presenting this new idea of yours as the main idea of an essay. This step in the process typically breaks down into three stages: planning, drafting, and revising.

PLANNING: To effectively explain a complex main idea, you need to lay out your thinking in detail and present readers with plenty of information. The more clearly you organize your information into meaningful patterns, the more likely it is that your readers will see how all those details work together to explain your main idea.

When someone throws a lot of disorganized information at you, you become confused. You don't see what all the information adds up to — if anything — and you gradually stop paying attention. To keep this from happening with your readers, you need to carefully inventory all the pieces of the information you plan to include in your essay and then arrange them according to an appropriate pattern.

One excellent tool to help you with this is a topic sentence outline. For each paragraph that you plan to write, you summarize the purpose of that paragraph in a single, complete sentence. You then arrange those topic sentences so that the order of presentation makes sense. It might be chronological, for example, or it might move from most to least important idea.

When confronted with the idea of a topic sentence outline, the more honest student writers will tell me that they never outline an essay. They just write from a mental outline. With a simple, short paper, that might work. Your mind might be large enough to do this. With a more complex paper, it probably won't work. To be sure you're making sense, take five minutes and briefly outline the information that helps to explain your main idea. Five minutes! It takes less time than flossing your teeth, and it won't make your gums bleed.

DRAFTING: This is where you put onto paper the actual words that will transfer an idea from your brain into the brains of your readers. Some writers can draft entire essays in their heads and then type them out as final drafts. These writers are so rare, however, that the federal government pays scientists to study them. I'm serious. If nobody's studying you, then you are probably not one of these writers. You should plan on writing more than one draft.

A good way to start is to draft just the body of your essay. Student writers often get hung up on achieving the perfect opening line. However, to write the perfect opening line, or even an okay opening line, you need to know what's in the body of the essay. A better starting point, then, is the body of the essay. So write a full paragraph for each point in your topic sentence outline. If you have to expand more important or complex points into multiple paragraphs, then do so. Another option is to write a quick, brief draft of the body and then expand upon and revise that draft until you remove the ineffective and irrelevant bits of information and include enough of the right stuff. There are many different methods for this step, but the end result should be a set of paragraphs that all work together to present and defend one main idea. Once the body is done, drafting a good opening and closing is much easier.

Drafting often leads you to unexpected discoveries about your topic, your idea, or yourself. Drafting relies on the subconscious mind to gather up the right words, and the subconscious mind, once activated, is creative and unpredictable — kind of like a four-year-old. You might discover that you need to go back to your topic and take another look at what the information really tells you. You might notice a new wrinkle in the information, and that might lead you to an even better main idea. You might also see that a big chunk of information in your essay isn't actually relevant to your particular idea. You might have to junk it. If drafting shows you that you have to make changes, then make changes. Don't fall too deeply in love with what you've written. It's just an essay, after all.

REVISING: This word can be used to describe any point at which you go back to an earlier step in the process and improve your idea, your organization, or your sentences. Revising in its broadest sense means "re-seeing." I have no quarrel with that broad use of the word, but that's not how it's used here. For our purposes, revision is primarily a matter of stepping back from your draft to polish it up for your audience.

You might introduce your main idea more colorfully in the opening, for example, or add or subtract bits of information to more effectively explain your idea. You might add a rebuttal to possible objections that others might have to your idea. You might remove that paragraph about your ingrown toenail as a metaphor for anarchy. In polishing your essay, you might even stumble upon a better idea and thus face more drastic choices.

Revision includes working on the mechanics of the essay, but save most of that until after you are confident of your idea and the body of the essay. You don't want to spend time worrying about how to spell "accommodate" or where to put a comma when the whole paragraph needs to be pulled out of the essay like a rank weed. You also don't want to lock in weak or irrelevant paragraphs of information by polishing up the punctuation. When you invest a lot of time in polishing garbage, the garbage starts to look pretty good. But it's still garbage.

Feedback is an important part of revision. Because your essay is trying to move from your brain and into the brain of another human, it helps to try out the essay on other humans, such as your professor, an editing group, a smart friend, and so on. This helps you check to see if the idea transfers successfully to other brains. Don't ask people if they like your essay. That doesn't matter, and anyway, most of them will say that they like it so that you will stop bothering them. Instead, ask them what they think your main idea is. If they can tell you, and if it *is* your main idea, then you've written a good essay because the main idea made its way successfully into their brains.

Student writers sometimes find it difficult to open up to

feedback. They think that criticism of something they've written is criticism of their intelligence. But it's not like that. What you've written is just that — something you've written. It's not you. It's not your intelligence. It's just an essay, an artifact of where you are right now as a writer. And even if it is pretty good, it's not as good as your essays will be with more practice.

Once you understand that your essay is just this thing you did, like the plastic ice scraper you made in eighth-grade shop class — which by the way was a pretty decent ice scraper — it becomes a lot easier to accept and benefit from the feedback of others.

Making the Process Work for You

In the end, and in seeming contradiction to the start of this chapter, you *will* have to discover a writing process that works specifically for you. This is the work of your brain, after all, and no two brains are alike. Brains, in this regard, are like snowflakes.

You should start with the three-step process of educating yourself about your topic, identifying and improving one main idea about that topic, and presenting your idea to others. This is generally how the writing process works for everyone. It's been working this way for thousands of years, and there's no reason to think that will change in your lifetime. As you get comfortable with this process, however, you should adapt and refine it so that it works best for your particular situation and habits.

You might find that the hardest step for you is narrowing your focus to one small part of your topic, and that talking to your friends — regardless of how little they actually know about your topic — is a great help. So be it. Good for you. Adapt the process to include them if that's what it takes to get you moving forward.

You might find that having your own special writing place is important, or that noise levels are a factor. You might need music or complete silence. You might need to turn off the television. You might need to boldly reclaim those vanilla-scented candles if they really do help you. It's good to figure these things out. Respect those discoveries and revise your writing process to include those conditions and precautions — but only if they don't get in the way of you thinking for yourself.

If you try to use this three-step writing process and it doesn't go anywhere for you, don't panic and above all don't go back to any inadequate processes from the past. Instead, talk to your writing professor. Most writing professors collect tricks for jump-starting writers at various stages of the writing process. It's a hobby they picked up in graduate school. If you don't have a writing professor, you can always search the Internet with this key phrase: "the writing process." A lot of what you find will be junk, of course, but you might also find just the right trick to get started.

CHAPTER 3
EDUCATE YOURSELF ABOUT YOUR TOPIC

Many students treat a writing assignment like it's a mild illness, something to get over as quickly as possible so that it won't interfere with any weekend plans. As soon as they receive an assignment, they jump to the first obvious idea that comes to mind and crank out an essay without a second thought. They don't care about learning anything new. All they want from their essay is for it to be finished — and the sooner the better. I've had students actually *brag* to me that they never spend more than forty-five minutes on an essay.

Foolish student writers!

First of all, stop bragging about how little time you invest in your professor's class. Your professors might outwardly scoff at such bravado, but inwardly they are weeping.

Second, and more importantly, please understand that your education is not an inconvenience, nor are your writing assignments blemishes on an otherwise happy life. Each writing assignment is in fact a generous invitation from your professor to spend some quality time with a new topic. Instead of giving you a lousy multiple-choice exam that will be graded by a machine, your professor has thoughtfully assigned your class an essay in the hope that at least a few of you will take this opportunity to actually get to know this new topic and discover new ideas for yourselves — to develop an understanding that will outlast this assignment and possibly even your time in college.

Later, when the math and psychology professors stand around the ScanTron machine, yukking it up while the machine grades their midterms, your professor will be loading up a painfully heavy briefcase with your essays, taking them home to read at a small desk in the laundry room while the rest of the family watches television or sleeps. It's a sacrifice of love, most fortunate student writer, and your professor is willing to make that sacrifice because he or she cares about your education.

However you might misunderstand or abuse it, your education is here for one purpose only — to make you a better person, a more thoughtful participant in the world. That's it. Even if your immediate purpose is vocational training, your classes are still trying to teach you to be a better listener, thinker, and communicator, to look at things from outside your own perspective, to respond to new topics and new challenges thoughtfully. Your education is trying to help you develop into something interesting and responsible, and it does this important work one topic at a time.

You say you don't care about a particular topic? You think it's boring? That's because you don't yet understand why it matters to you. But your professor *does* understand and is trying to help you to see that for yourself with this writing assignment. And you will see it, too. All you have to do is receive the assignment as it was intended, as an opportunity to examine one small part of the world more closely and then share your discoveries.

Most of this book focuses on the "share your discoveries" part of the process, which in this case is writing a college essay. However, the college essay is really just a byproduct of the more important work of educating yourself about your topic. So before we work on how to share your ideas, we'll first look at how to educate yourself about your topic. We'll start with strategies for getting to know the topic. We'll then look at how to use questions to narrow your focus and consider more detailed information.

GETTING TO KNOW YOUR TOPIC

You begin the process of self-education by getting to know your topic. You usually start by gathering some basic information. With most classes, you've already started to gather information about your topic by the time you receive a writing assignment. If you're taking American History, for example, you might be given a new topic to write about — Benjamin Franklin in Paris — but you've been learning about a lot of related topics from those Revolutionary times, so you're not completely unfamiliar with Franklin, Paris, or the relationship of the Colonial and French governments. What you already know will give you a few ideas about where you can gather more specific information about Franklin in Paris. But if you're not sure where to start, you also have a handy resource just standing there, idly, at the front of the classroom. Raise your hand, thank your professor for the assignment (in a sincere voice), and then ask for a few starting points for your research.

Begin with Reference Works

Outside of the classroom, the best way to get started with a topic is to use general reference works. These are publications that are typically written by experts for an audience of non-experts. A dictionary is the most common general source of information. It explains all the words in a language — or at least all the words that will not make your mother blush. A medical or legal dictionary explains all the terms or topics within that somewhat narrower focus. Encyclopedias are also common general sources. General encyclopedias attempt to briefly explain *everything*. Topical encyclopedias — an encyclopedia of religion or zoology or history, for example — are just as ambitious within the boundaries of that topic. Textbooks are another general source you should consider. They're good at explaining important terms related to the topic and providing a comprehensive overview. Textbooks are also good at presenting the debatable issues within your topic — any of which might become an avenue for deeper exploration.

The Internet is home to many useful reference works, but you can't just visit two or three websites and assume that you've mastered the topic. You've only scratched the surface of the topic, and what you've scratched could be garbage, too, depending on the two or three websites you visit. Using the Internet wisely means learning how to find credible websites and judging the reliability of any information you find. The reliability usually comes down to two factors: the credentials of the authors and the objectivity of the information.

With printed reference works, for example, the reliability is usually high. That's because dictionaries and encyclopedias are expensive to create. They require significant funding and a lot of coordination, so if it's ever going to happen, the work will be done by qualified professionals. Any printed dictionary, for example, is the work of professional scholars, and the same will be true of topical dictionaries and encyclopedias. Many online sources are also the careful work of trained professionals. Government websites are produced by agency professionals who understand their subject areas well. Many printed publications provide electronic versions of the same publication, and these are just as credible as the printed versions.

With some websites, however, the website's users create the content — book reviews, travel guides, dining reviews, technical help. These sites are less reliable because the writers are less credible. With a book review site, for example, the author of a review *might* be qualified to judge the quality of a book. But the reviewer might also be the still-angry former girlfriend of the author. Or he might be an intern working for the book's publisher. Or she might be an elderly Lutheran who never rates anything highly because she doesn't want to encourage too much self-esteem. User-generated sites rarely use editors to screen out dumb or biased reviews, so you have to be more careful judging the objectivity of each review. You can learn a lot at these sites, but you need to test what you learn with more objective sources.

In the case of the world's most famous online encyclopedia, Wikipedia, the content is provided by users, but there are several levels of editorial review and often fierce debate among competing viewpoints. That editorial review, along with citations of sources and a generally more informed and professional set of contributors, makes this online encyclopedia much more reliable than many grumpy old professors are willing to admit. It's still possible for any idiot to corrupt an article with silly information — "Dogs are cats. Cats are dogs." — but that kind of silliness is quickly removed.

The second quality to look for when it comes to reliability is objective information. That means you can actually see the details of the information — the facts of the matter, the real-world particulars — and not just summaries or someone's opinion about what the information means. Because the scope of a reference work is so broad, reference works rely on summaries and key pieces of information rather than details. Because the writers of these sources are usually credible professionals, you can trust those summaries more than if they came from the users of a website, but they're still mostly summaries rather than detailed pieces of information.

Reference works will help you understand the basics of your topic, teach you the relevant terminology, and identify points of interest or debate that will be worth a closer look. However, to really understand a topic, you'll have to narrow your focus and dig deeper to find more detailed information.

IF YOUR TOPIC IS A TEXT, TRY READING IT

If the assigned topic is a piece of writing — a poem, an essay by Kierkegaard, an article in the journal *Nature* — you have to start by actually reading it. That sounds pretty obvious, doesn't it? Please keep that in mind when you're tempted to turn to SparkNotes or Google instead of just reading the text for yourself. Your professor assigned that text because he or she thinks you'll benefit from a better understanding of it, so perhaps you should trust your professor's judgment this one time and get to know the text first-hand.

Reading the text once will help you to become acquainted with the topic, just as reading from reference works will help you to become acquainted with other topics. The thing about a text, though, is that reading it once only gives you an acquaintance, not an understanding. In fact, you really need to read it twice just to become well acquainted.

As you go through the text — both times — make a few notes about things you notice. These might be great lines that you like, confusing phrases, information or events that don't make any sense, or anything else that stands out for you. When you can, try to state your notes as questions. Don't try to figure out the answers to all these questions while you're reading. Just make notes so that you can later return to those questions and use them to narrow your focus within the text.

NARROWING YOUR FOCUS

Narrowing your focus means looking more closely at a smaller part of your topic. This is how you really get to know a topic, by exploring its complexities more deeply. However, you can't explore *all* the complexities — there's never enough time for that — so you have to pick something that engages you and leave the other, equally engaging parts of the topic for another time. By "another time," of course, I mean "probably never."

As you get to know your topic, you'll find yourself drawn toward certain interesting or debatable or strange subtopics and questions. If you start with the broad topic of the United States' Bill of Rights, for example, you might find yourself drawn to the Fifth Amendment — particularly the final "takings" clause. That would be worth deeper exploration. Or if you are assigned the somewhat troubling topic of "mime," you might discover that Charlie Chaplin — whom you love — studied mime before becoming a film star. This raises the question of just how much Chaplin's film performances rely on mime techniques. That would be worth a closer look, too.

You might be drawn to these smaller parts of the topic because others have been interested before you and have written a lot about it. That makes it easier to educate yourself about that smaller part. You might be drawn to them for personal reasons as you find intersections between the topic and your own experience. You might be drawn to them — for reasons you don't understand — by your subconscious mind or the forces of the universe. It doesn't really matter how you get there. Just get there.

Once you find a narrower focus, you should more or less ignore the rest of the topic and become an expert in that one area. Doing that improves the odds of your essay becoming thoughtful, detailed, and engaging to readers. If you have any doubts about the appropriateness of a narrowed focus for an assignment, talk to your professor. Otherwise, just have fun finding and understanding the more complex information that you will discover within these narrower boundaries.

With some writing assignments, you're assigned a question rather than a topic. This typically happens when the class has already spent plenty of time with a general topic and your professor now wants you to dig deeper into the information that's available. In this case, your professor has narrowed the focus for you. You still need to spend some time getting to know that topic in general, but once that's been done you can get right to work educating yourself about this narrowed focus.

It may be that after gathering information about a topic, you really don't have any questions. Nothing looks weird because it *all* looks weird — because it's all new information, in other words. In that case, you can use one of many writerly tricks such as free-writing or mind-mapping to better explore the topic. Free-writing is writing nonstop for fifteen or twenty minutes to see what your subconscious mind can come up with. We're all so repressed that there's usually several interesting observations or questions ready to escape from your brain. Mind-mapping is using a chart of some sort to visually divide a topic into its many subtopics — and then sub-subtopics and sub-sub-subtopics. This helps you identify interesting patterns or components that might be worth a closer examination.

Another useful device is the reporter's questions, the six questions that any good journalist will ask to explore a topic: Who? What? When? Where? Why? and How? The reporter's questions help you explore and understand the specifics of your topic, and that process almost always raises additional questions that will lead you to further exploration.

WHO? Who is doing this? To whom is it being done? Who else is affected? You can think of this question as identifying the actors in a drama. The drama is your topic, and the actors are the forces at work within that topic. The actors involved might be human or they might also be broader forces at work (unemployment, inflation) or groups (the NRA, unruly schoolchildren) or nations or ideas — anyone or anything that might do something or cause something to happen.

WHAT? What happened? What is happening? What is going to happen? These might be physical, observable events or internal, unobservable events. Think about change with this question. What changed? What is changing? What will change? One technique here is to take each of the answers to "Who?" and look for some verbs that go with each noun (*unemployment* increases incidents of spousal abuse, *the NRA* lobbies against gun registration).

WHEN? This might be a specific time or date. It might also be the set of conditions that must be present for an event to happen, like the circumstances that must be present for the stock market to crash or for a yucca plant to bloom.

WHERE? This question can look at actual physical locations in which an event might take place — the city, the house, the sandbox where the cat has been seen digging. However, it also considers less tangible contexts, such as the country music scene, the Internet, or the fast food industry.

WHY? What causes this to happen? This is one of the more useful questions because it forces you to start figuring out why your "who" actors are doing the "what" actions, or why your "what" actions have such interesting consequences. You make more sense of the topic by considering the relationship of actors to other actors and events to other events. When you try to answer this question, use complete sentences that include the word "because." Using the word "because" forces you to at least guess about why something happens. And guessing is fine, too. It gives you ideas you can test with more detailed information about that smaller part of the topic.

How? This question looks at method, at how something happens. It's another good question that will help you to make connections and explore beneath the surface of a topic. Like "Why?" you should answer this question with complete sentences. Using the word "by" in your sentences will help you note or guess about the methods used by the actors.

By focusing on the particulars of a topic, the reporter's questions tend to generate deeper consideration than free-writing or mind-mapping. Doing this will almost always lead to questions or aspects of the topic that you hadn't thought of before. And that's where the fun begins.

Exploring the Narrowed Focus

Once you've narrowed your focus, the next step is to set aside the reference works and turn toward more detailed sources of information. These include books, serious popular magazines, newspapers, and scholarly journals. These sources offer more comprehensive information than reference works, so they allow you to educate yourself about your newly narrowed topic more thoroughly.

You will find a few of these resources online and available to the general public, but the best way for student writers to get their hands on serious and scholarly information is through a college or university library. Campus libraries now use electronic databases to catalog their resources, so you can find what you need using key word searches — not unlike how you look for information with an Internet search engine.

Turn Questions Into Key Word Searches

To find more comprehensive information from library databases, you need to search for it using key words. The key words will come from the questions you have. Suppose you have this question: "Did Ben Franklin contract syphilis while serving as an American diplomat in Paris?" To create a list of key words for your search, you simply circle the important words in your question — Ben Franklin, syphilis, American diplomat, Paris. You then search for books or articles by typing some or all of those terms into a database search page.

That's your starting point, and that might be all you have to do to find the information you need about Franklin's sexual activity. However, you might also find that those terms generate a list of a thousand articles, which is more than you have time to review, or that those articles are only loosely related to the American diplomat. On the other hand, you might also find that searching for those terms gives you a list of zero possible sources. That seems pretty unlikely with some topics and some questions, but it happens all the time if the key words you use aren't the same ones that the database uses.

One way to improve your search is to try using synonyms for some of your terms. Instead of "diplomat," you could use "statesman," "ambassador," or "envoy." Instead of "American," you could use "Colonial" or "Colonial American." By trying different synonyms, you often stumble upon the key words that best fit your topic from the database's perspective. Write those down so you can keep using them.

Your best friend for generating useful key words will be the Library of Congress's guide to subject headings. You can find this multivolume resource in your local college library and online — as I'm writing this, anyway — at this elegant web address: **id.loc.gov**. This is the list of the official key words used by almost all search engines, so if you can find the right words here, your key word searches are likely to be much more successful. A recent student, for example, said he was doing research about exotic dancers, but he couldn't find any scholarly articles using the terms "exotic dancers," "strippers," or anything else he could think of. When he went to the Library of Congress Subject Headings, he found that the official term was "stripteasers." Who'd have thought it? When he used "stripteasers," he found 40 years worth of scholarly data, which was also a surprise.

Another thing you can try — especially if your search yields little or nothing — is to use broader categories in place of some of your search terms. Instead of "syphilis," for example, you might use "sexually transmitted diseases" or "venereal disease" to enlarge your search. Instead of "Paris" you might search for "France" or "Europe." In this way, you will sometimes find articles with a broader scope that also include some information about your question. Your new friend, the Library of Congress's list of subject headings, is ready to help with this task, too. Not only will it offer you the official key words, it will also offer the official, broader categories to which those key words belong. Isn't that nice of it? This is also how you can find books that are relevant to your question. They are almost always going to be more broadly focused than you need simply because of their length. However, within those books you might find chapters or parts of chapters that will be useful.

BUILD YOUR UNDERSTANDING WITH SERIOUS POPULAR PUBLICATIONS

When you search your library's databases for scholarly information, the results will be much better than when you search the Internet. When you look at the results, there won't be any defunct websites in the mix. There won't be any ads for free laptops or baldness remedies or attractive singles in your area. When you search for information at the library, that's exactly what you'll find — information — and most of it will be reliable because librarians have no patience for unreliable information. They weed it out for you like angry badgers.

As you begin reading the articles that you've located, it's a good idea to start with the more serious popular sources on your list. These articles come from magazines and newspapers written for broad audiences of readers who are educated but not experts in a particular field. The magazines and newspapers that print these articles are there to make money, and they make their money by targeting popular issues and exploring them thoughtfully. This brings more educated readers to their pages, and it allows the publications to sell advertising to businesses that want to reach readers with higher levels of education and — usually — higher levels of income.

However, don't confuse these serious popular publications with the far more popular and far less serious publications that focus on the sad lives of glamorous celebrities or how to make your wedding even more expensive. The role of these publications is primarily to make plane flights seem shorter or to give you something to do while waiting to see a dentist. They are trying to entertain as many readers as possible so they can sell advertising to businesses trying to reach lots of readers all at once. That's fine. I have nothing against entertainment or advertising. But when it comes to educating yourself about a topic, the serious popular sources have more to offer.

Newspapers are the most common type of serious popular publication. They rely on professional journalists to gather information from credible sources, to confirm the validity of that information, and to present that information objectively. They cover a wide array of events, usually in brief articles. With compelling or controversial events, they might explore the details in more depth, including information from scholars, local authorities, and others who have a professional relationship to the topic.

Not all newspapers are credible, of course. Tabloid papers, for example, often ignore real-world information and print speculation and suspicion — knuckleheads! They also like to focus on the lurid details that appeal to the latent fears and lusts of their audience. That's why they're so popular. Small-town papers tend to focus on gentle human-interest stories about their readers — and kittens! — so that those same gentle humans will renew their subscriptions. That's really sweet of the small-town papers to do that, but it's not too useful when it comes to educating yourself about a even a local topic.

The reason that serious popular sources are so useful is that they translate the detailed work of scholars into language that ordinary, educated people can understand. That means you can become more knowledgeable about the details of your topic without having to become a scholar yourself. Magazine and newspaper articles are also more focused on smaller parts of the topic than general reference works. That means they can provide more detailed and often more timely information. These articles are thus a great way for you to wade into those details and prepare you for your next step in the self-education process — some scholarly reading.

DEEPEN YOUR UNDERSTANDING WITH SCHOLARLY PUBLICATIONS

At the deep end of the information pool, you will find articles and books that are written by scholars, edited by scholars, and, for the most part, read by scholars. Scholarly writers are the most credible because they are both knowledgeable about their field and they're trained in methods of gathering and testing information within that field. Moreover, when a scholar submits an article or book for publication, other scholars are hired to examine that submission, judge its value, and sniff out even the smallest flaws, just itching for some reason to reject it. Anything that does get published has to hold up well to that kind of mean-spirited scrutiny.

The more important factor, however, is that scholarly work focuses most directly on the details of information. This allows readers to see those details for themselves and then form their own conclusions about what it means or try to replicate the results. These details are measurable facts rather than the summary or interpretation of facts that show up in popular magazines. They are quotations from and references to primary texts, the quantifiable results of experiments or studies, the exact words of interviewees. They connect the conclusions of scholars to the real world, and that's what makes this information more objective and useful.

For all their virtues, however, scholarly sources have one major drawback. Scholars write these articles for other scholars. They don't mess around trying to explain things to newbies like you. They assume that their readers are familiar with the topic and the terminology of their discipline. If you're not familiar with the topic or terminology — and there's a good chance you're not, student writer — you will find scholarly sources difficult to figure out. That's not a reason to avoid them, however. That's a reason to be patient with your climb up the learning curve. It's also a reason to go back to your general sources (especially dictionaries) for help decoding difficult articles and books.

WHY NARROW IS BETTER

At first, you might not feel comfortable narrowing the focus of your research. It does, after all, violate the simple math of high school report writing — size of topic = length of report. However, here's one of those writerly paradoxes for you. As it turns out, a broad focus actually tends to limit the writer and generate a dull and shorter-than-expected essay. This happens because the broad range of information required by a big topic forces you to rely on summarized rather than detailed information. Summaries can be written quickly, and by "quickly" I mean with fewer words. They also tend to be less vivid, particularly when they stand alone without details to illustrate them. By "less vivid," I mean boring. Thus you end up with a short and dull essay.

Suppose that your topic is math and your essay answers this question: How important is math in daily life? With a focus like this, you'll need to include a book-sized amount of information because almost every aspect of daily life has a direct or indirect connection to math. You might offer a few detailed examples (balancing a checkbook, figuring out what kind of mileage your SUV gets, and so on), but the examples won't adequately explain your answer to the question because they cover only a small part of daily life. To answer the question fully, you'll need to cover most or all of the math-related aspects of daily life, and that will require summaries of the broad range of information that's needed. You'll end up with paragraphs that look like this:

> Math is also important in household activities. Math may be used to balance the checkbook and make budgets. It might also be used to determine the cost of vacations or weekend trips. It can be used when shopping to compare the relative cost of similar products and help determine the most economical product to purchase. With just about every household activity, math is close at hand.

The summaries in that paragraph cover a lot of information quickly, but that doesn't help you get the length you need. More importantly, they don't spark your imagination or provide any sparks for your readers. So while the old principle of report-writing still works — the broader the focus, the more information you have to work with — covering more information doesn't usually result in a longer essay or better main idea.

When you start to narrow your focus, you remove information from consideration, and that's a good thing because it allows you to get into the details of the information. By narrowing "How important is math in daily life?" to "How important is geometry in daily life?" you eliminate from consideration all forms of math except geometry. By narrowing your focus further to "How important is plane geometry in residential construction?" you remove most of the original topic and finally get into some detailed information. You might explore how the Pythagorean theorem, for example, is used by framing carpenters to make sure walls are laid out square:

> One common use of plane geometry occurs whenever a framing carpenter needs to plan where to put the walls of a house. It's essential that the walls are square (that is, with the junction of walls forming true right angles). This makes the work of drywallers and finish carpenters much easier because they will be able to make all their cuts quickly without having to take the time to compensate for walls and corners that aren't square. To make sure the walls are all laid out square, the framer uses the Pythagorean theorem: $A^2 + B^2 = C^2$. If Wall A, for example, is 30 feet long, then A^2 will be 900. If Wall B is 40 feet long, then B^2 will be 1600. If Wall A and Wall B are joined at a true right angle, then the distance from the far end of Wall A to the far end of Wall B will be the square root of the sum of 900 and 1600. The sum of 900 plus 1600 is 2500. The square root of 2500 is 50. If Wall A and Wall B are laid out square, the diagonal that connects their far ends would be 50 feet long. If the framer makes sure these lengths are true, the walls will be square.

If math gives you stomachaches, then this detailed example of math for the carpenter isn't going to do much for you — except give you a really bad stomachache. But even so, you can still appreciate how the specific information in this paragraph gets its narrow little point across much more clearly than you saw in the previous summary with its huge ideas. Here you have details that you can visualize in your mind.

If the length issue still bothers you, you can also appreciate that it took a lot of sentences to present these specific details. In fact, even though it does bring in details, this math paragraph is still a little rushed. It could have walked through the process in even more detail with the illustration of a hypothetical carpenter at work on a hypothetical house.

Exploring your narrowed focus is where educating yourself about your topic offers the greatest rewards. In fact, this thoughtful consideration of detailed information offers the only meaningful reward you're going to get from a writing assignment. The essay you eventually write will come and go. The grade will become unimportant almost immediately. But when you take the time to really educate yourself about your topic, that topic will stay with you — especially the part of the topic that you explore more deeply.

As an added bonus, narrowing your focus will also prepare you to write an engaging and effective essay. Because you understand the topic so well — especially within your narrowed focus — length won't be a problem for you. You'll be able to find an idea of your own that will be worth sharing with readers, and you'll be able to share that idea with sophisticated explanations and detailed information.

CHAPTER 4

FIND AND IMPROVE YOUR MAIN IDEA

Once you get used to the process of educating yourself about a topic, you'll find that gathering and considering information becomes surprisingly enjoyable. As you spend time with the information and then dig deeper into that topic, you begin to understand it in more than just a superficial way. You make discoveries you weren't expecting, discoveries that you can't help but share with others.

This is particularly true when the assigned topic or question isn't something you would have chosen for yourself. The dull exterior of the topic opens to reveal unexpected complexities you wouldn't have otherwise noticed. These discoveries are ideas of your own — not facts, and not summaries of information. You will be able to use one of them as the main idea of your essay. This chapter shows you how to identify and then improve an idea of your own before you start writing. The only problem that might prevent you from making the most of these ideas would be your own unwillingness to practice the ideas from Chapter 3.

With a college essay, you need to know what you're writing about. You can't fake it anymore. To write a good essay, you really do have to give thanks for the assignment as an opportunity to educate yourself about one more topic. Then you have to do the work of educating yourself. That's the pathway to understanding, and understanding is required for a good essay. That's also the requirement for identifying and refining the main idea of your essay. If you don't know what you're talking about, you won't be able to improve your main idea.

I'll go ahead and explain how to identify and improve a main idea, student writer, but I'm telling you right now that it won't be any use to you unless you also understand and adopt the ideas from Chapter 3.

FINDING A LEGITIMATE MAIN IDEA

To write a college essay, you first need to know what your main idea will be, and you need to know this precisely. You can't *kind of* know. If you only *kind of* know what your idea is, then your readers will only *kind of* know what you mean. Transmitting a vague understanding in an essay is not to be confused with success. It will lead to confused readers and comments from your professor such as, "I'm not sure what you mean by this" and "D."

The best way to identify and refine the main idea of your future essay is to put it into words and then refine it as a more precise and accurate idea. To do this, you need to use something that writing professors call "the thesis statement." You remember this term from Chapter 1, provided of course that you read Chapter 1. A thesis statement will look something like this:

> People should try to laugh when they feel stressed out, even if it's fake laughter, because any kind of laughter will help to reduce stress.

Notice that this thesis statement is a complete sentence, that it defines an opinion of your own (advice is always an opinion), and that it includes a reason why your readers should follow the advice. You need a complete sentence to have a complete thought. A "because" phrase is an added bonus since it gives a reason why readers should accept your idea. It also defines what sort of information will be needed to explain and perhaps defend your idea.

You might remember the thesis statement from your days of writing five-paragraph trainer-essays. Back in those dark times, the thesis statement was the last sentence of the first paragraph, the sentence that stated that your essay would have three main points to make. We're not talking about that out-dated kind of a thesis statement. The old thesis statement was merely a summary of the essay's contents — child's play.

The college-essay kind of thesis statement is a definition of your essay's main idea — the insightful opinion that you will be sharing with others. To define that idea precisely, you need a thesis statement that will be far too cumbersome to actually insert into your essay. This kind of thesis statement is a writer's tool. Your readers will never see it.

The writerly thesis statement works behind the scenes to help you capture and improve your main idea while your thoughts are still fluid. It will give you a clearer purpose before you start to write, and it will guide you while you write. This will lead to more successful papers, better grades, higher paying jobs, and ultimately an expensive boat that you will rarely find time to enjoy. In spite of these obvious rewards for using a writerly thesis statement, many student writers view the thesis statement as a complete waste of time. Wouldn't it be easier, they think, to just write the paper once they have a general direction and all the information is still fresh?

Foolish student writers! It only *seems* like a complete waste of time because the quality of your thinking has never mattered before. It matters now. The quality of a college essay depends on the quality of your own ideas, not on your ability to collect information. The thesis statement captures your thinking in advance, and by improving that sentence, you can fix the any weaknesses in your idea before your weak idea turns into a dumb essay. This makes the thesis statement one of most valuable tools you have as a writer.

Starting is often the hardest step in using the thesis statement to identify and improve an idea. It's hard to write a single sentence that clearly states your main idea. It's much easier to write a paragraph or two. It's even easier to leave a vague notion floating around in your brain waves. Consequently, there is a tendency among student writers to work on main ideas "mentally," often while watching television or sleeping. However, one of the great writerly secrets is that *any* starting point is a good starting point. Once you've written a sentence — even a lousy one — you can tinker with it to make it better, and tinkering is easier than starting. Take this lousy starting point, for example:

the stress-reducing benefits of laughter

laughing your way to a brighter tomorrow

The reason these are lousy is that they are still phrases rather than complete sentences. If what you write down is a phrase rather than a complete sentence, then even if it's a nice little phrase, you have a statement of a topic or subtopic rather than a complete idea. These phrases tell readers what you will be writing about, but they don't state your own conclusion about the topic. To state your opinion, you'll need a complete sentence. That's not hard to do. Try again:

Will laughter reduce your stress?

I probably should have mentioned that when I say "complete sentence," I don't mean a question, even though that's also a complete sentence. Questions ask for ideas. They don't present them. The *answer* to this question might be a reasonable opinion of your own, but to capture that thought, you'll need to state an assertion rather than a question. Try again:

I think that laughter probably reduces stress.

That's a complete sentence. It's a statement rather than a question. The statement also captures a discovery of yours, which is good. But look at the subject of the sentence — "I." "I" implies that this is an idea about you and that you are having a thought. The "I think" also suggests that you are qualifying this idea by saying that it's just your opinion, that this seems true to you but you really don't want to get into a big fight over it.

College writing, however, requires you to present an opinion of your own, so whenever someone reads your essay, the "I think" is already understood. Your idea in that essay must also be more than just a hunch of yours, an idea that shouldn't have to be qualified by a wimpy "I think." This needs to be an opinion that is reasonable, that is based on the information you found and considered when you were exploring your topic. It needs to be an idea that makes sense not just to you but to anyone who looks at the information.

So try again, emboldened student writer, and this time let your topic become the subject of the sentence:

Laughter probably reduces stress.

Much better! Now you have a complete sentence. It's an assertion of your own idea. It focuses on a specific topic. This is a big step forward. You've identified a potential main idea for an essay. In a minute we'll look at how to improve that idea before you write the essay. First, though, we'll look at some thesis statements that will lead to reports rather than essays.

If what you write down is a sentence that summarizes information or states a fact about the topic, then even though it is a complete sentence and not a question, it's not a good main idea for an essay. Consider these examples:

Laughter is a regular part of human life.

Most people have some degree of stress.

These are both statements, but they are statements of fact rather than opinion. We already know these things. We don't disagree. If you write about these ideas, you'll be writing a report about information rather than an essay about your interpretation of what that information means. And you're not much better off with an opinion that is obvious, like this:

Laughter is a great gift.

That's not a fact or a summary of information, so the paper that explains this idea *would* be an essay. However, this idea is so simple that any ten-year-old could figure it out — if ten-year-olds didn't have better things to do, anyway. The essay that explains this idea, even if it's technically excellent, would have little to offer its readers.

USING A THESIS STATEMENT TO IMPROVE YOUR MAIN IDEA

The way to improve your main idea — to make sure it's worthy of the essay you're about to write — is to improve your writerly thesis statement. You will use the thesis statement to make your thinking more precise, and you will use it to make sure that the idea is accurate. Let's take that idea you had about laughter as an example:

Laughter probably reduces stress.

To make an idea more precise, you need to define the key terms of the thesis statement more clearly. So what do you mean by "laughter"? What do you mean by "stress"? What do you mean by "reduces"? Try to be more precise:

All types of laughter will probably lower the levels of emotional stress that people feel.

That's better. Now we know you're talking about all laughter, including feigned laughter. We also see that you're focusing on the emotional stress that people feel, rather than physical or spiritual or other kinds of stress. But what about "lower"? How much lower? What did the information tell you about this?

If your answer to a question like this is "I don't know," then you have a problem that you need to take seriously. If you don't know what you mean, then you don't have any business presenting this idea. You're not informed enough to do that. You're just guessing. Either you need to go back to your topic and educate yourself more thoroughly, or you need to move on to another idea of yours that is not dependent on guesswork.

And by the way, indignant student writer, it's a lousy excuse to say that the source you were using didn't tell you how much the stress was reduced. It probably didn't go into the details because it was a general reference article or a magazine article. Remember that general sources of information stick more to the surface of a topic. When you run into sources that aren't as detailed as you need them to be, it's *your* job to find that more detailed information. You know it's out there because the writers of the general sources were able to find it and summarize it. So go find the information and then come back with a new thesis statement:

> All types of laughter will probably lower the levels of emotional stress that people feel by 20-30%.

Good job with the follow-up research. Now you know more precisely what you mean by "lower." But that "probably" still needs to be considered. I'll go out on a limb and say it's in the sentence because you know that this isn't always true. There are exceptions to this rule, and "probably" covers those exceptions without you having to articulate them. That was nice of "probably" to save you that effort, but it leaves your sentence imprecise. So replace the "probably" with a statement that includes the exceptions to this idea. Try again:

> Except in the cases of severely depressed people, all types of laughter other than hysterical or feigned laughter will lower the levels of emotional stress that people feel by 20-30%.

That's much more precise than the thesis statement you started with, and that precision will really help you as you plan and then write your essay. Before you get to the planning and writing, however, you still have to make sure that this idea is accurate. That means testing whether the idea you're asserting in this thesis statement is founded on sufficient reasons or information. The quickest way to test this is to add the word "because" to your sentence and then summarize what leads you to believe this idea is valid. Try it for yourself:

> Except in the cases of severely depressed people, all types of laughter other than hysterical or feigned laughter will lower the levels of emotional stress that people feel by 20-30% because laughter has been shown to release powerful mood-enhancing chemicals into the bloodstream.

Before we get to accuracy, let's go back to precision for a moment. When you write something like "has been shown to release," you're hiding whatever studies have shown this to be true. To judge the accuracy of your idea, you need to be precise about this supporting information, too. You might as well name the chemicals while you're at it. Try again:

> Except in the cases of severely depressed people, all types of laughter other than hysterical or feigned laughter will lower the levels of emotional stress that people feel by 20-30% because two recent Purdue studies showed that an hour of regular laughter releases up to 100 milligrams of serotonin into the bloodstream.

That's more precise. Thank you. And now you can test your idea for accuracy. Does the information you have sufficiently support the idea? That's a tough question to answer when you're just starting out as a writer of college essays. It takes practice to learn how to judge how well evidence supports your ideas, so don't be surprised if your answer to this question is more of a blank stare or a furrowed brow. With practice and feedback from others, though, you'll begin to see for yourself how this works.

One way to judge whether your information provides enough support is to turn that sentence into a kind of math problem. Imagine that the "because" is an equals sign. Does the idea that you state before the "because" equal the information or reasons that you state after the "because"? If it does, then your statement is accurate. If it doesn't, then you need to tinker with one or both sides of the equation so that the idea and its support are equal.

With this sentence, the question is whether those two Purdue studies about laughter and serotonin are strong enough information for this assertion about laughter. Do they *prove* that this idea is true? No, they don't. There are two problems. First, because they are just studies of a limited number of humans, all they can do is identify a pattern in those humans that *might* be true in all humans. Second, the studies are about the chemicals, not the stress, so the connection of serotonin to stress still needs to be made. The studies still are worth considering, but they don't prove that laughter will for a fact reduce stress except in certain circumstances.

One thing to do to make this more accurate is to make sure that the information is being presented as completely and as strongly as possible That means going back to your topic to see if you got it right. Maybe those Purdue studies are actually more convincing than you state here. Perhaps this is the truth:

> Except in the cases of severely depressed people, all types of laughter other than hysterical or feigned laughter will lower the levels of emotional stress that people feel by 20-30% because two recent Purdue studies confirmed a widely held theory that an hour of regular laughter releases up to 100 milligrams of serotonin into the bloodstream.

Okay. That's a bit more convincing. But what about connecting the serotonin to stress? Is there a connection? If so, can you include that in your support for your idea? Try again:

> Except in the cases of severely depressed people, all types of laughter other than hysterical or feigned laughter will lower the levels of emotional stress that people feel by 20-30% because two recent Purdue studies confirmed a widely held theory that an hour of regular laughter releases up to 100 milligrams of serotonin into the bloodstream and because the American Board of Psychiatry recommends serotonin enhancement as an effective way to reduce stress by 20-30%.

This more precise statement of the information and reasoning behind your idea shows that the support for this idea is stronger than it seemed at first. Now we can look at the idea that comes prior to the first "because" and test whether the information and reasoning that come after will sufficiently support it. What do you think?

Seriously?

No, I'm afraid that this assertion is still overstating its support. The statement at present says that except in the stated cases, laughter "*will* lower the levels of stress." That means this is a reliable fact of human experience. However, while it *might* be a fact of human experience, the support for the idea does not have the same broad focus. It doesn't examine a broad range of humans over a long period of time. It only shows that higher levels of serotonin have recently been produced among a select number of humans — or maybe monkeys — from Indiana.

The connection of serotonin to stress is also a little iffy. Yes, the American Board of Psychiatry's recommendation of serotonin to reduce stress does make the connection appear to be an idea that's worth taking seriously, but it doesn't make it a fact. The board's recommendations are suggestions that are also based on the best information available at the moment — educated guesses, in other words, that change as research continues and information improves.

So even though the information makes sense and suggests that laughter really is beneficial, you shouldn't take it too far by saying it proves something. It only suggests something. To make your statement of the idea accurate, then, you have to capture this suggestive nature of the supporting information:

> Except in the cases of severely depressed people, all types of laughter other than hysterical or feigned laughter may lower the levels of emotional stress that people feel by 20-30% because two recent Purdue studies confirmed a widely held theory that an hour of regular laughter releases up to 100 milligrams of serotonin into the bloodstream and because the American Board of Psychiatry recommends serotonin enhancement as an effective way to reduce stress by 20-30%.

That's much better. By changing "will" to "may," you've turned this idea from a fact into a possibility. It now appears that the idea is equal to its support. It's thus both precise and accurate.

Your thesis statement has come a long way in a short time, and you're ready now to start planning how to present your idea, using this thesis statement as your guide. We'll get to that in the next chapter. In the meantime, please remember that this sentence is just for you, the writer. You should write it on a little card and tape it to your computer while you're working on your essay. It's your essay's mission statement, for those of you who like mission statements. If your readers want to see this idea, they'll have to read the essay that accomplishes that mission.

Working so intently on one single sentence might feel difficult or overly time-consuming at first, but with a little practice you'll find that it's not really so hard if you start with a simple idea — even a lousy one. From there, you can clean it up and expand it into a complex idea. You just have to stay grounded in the information you've learned about your topic and return to that information whenever you need to be more precise and accurate.

I'll be honest. A lot of student writers blow this chapter off and launch into their essays like everything I've told them is a load of manure. "Thank you, Mr. English Teacher," they imply by their actions, "but I've been writing papers for years. I don't need your *writerly* thesis statements." They have more faith in their own ability to crank out essays without any planning than they do in the thesis statement's ability to prepare them to write thoughtful essays.

Foolish student writers! I understand that inspiration sometimes bails you out in spite of poor planning. Creative phrasing might decorate sloppy thinking just enough to make it appear thoughtful. A professor might read a stack of papers while watching a zombie movie, half-drunk, miserable for company, and in this way miss the fact that you haven't said anything worthwhile to share. Line up enough accidents of fate and you can get by without tinkering with a thesis statement.

However, you will eventually come to a place where you need to make sure your idea is precise and accurate before you present it in written form. It might not be a college essay, either. It might be a letter of resignation, a business plan, a scholarship application — something that needs to be taken seriously. When that day comes, remember this chapter. The thesis statement will still be a useful tool for you, and this chapter will still be here, too, reminding you how to use it — as long as you don't sell the book back to the bookstore at the end of the term.

CHAPTER 5

PLAN THE BODY OF YOUR ESSAY

For the moment, we'll ignore the opening and closing of your essay. Many student writers enjoy spending desperate hours staring at a blank computer screen, waiting for a perfect first line to appear from somewhere in the universe. If you enjoy staring at a blank computer screen, you still can, of course. It's peaceful. I get that. However, when it comes to writing your essay, it's a lot easier to write a great opening *after* you've written the body of the essay. By then, you will know what to introduce. You will also know what ideas and information you'll need to summarize in the closing. So for now, the opening and closing can wait.

In this chapter, you'll look at how to plan the body of your essay before you write it. You'll start out with a brief theory of paragraphs. Don't skip over or skim that section because you almost certainly need to relearn it. Then you'll see the options you have for arranging all the paragraphs that will be required to effectively explain your main idea.

A Brief Theory of Paragraphs

Most student writers create a new paragraph whenever they feel like it, and their feelings are guided not by ideas but by aesthetics. They look at the page and see that they have accumulated four or five lines of text. This worries them. They don't want the paper to look boring, so they say good-bye to the current paragraph and hello to a new one.

Foolish student writers!

A paragraph has a job to do. One part of that job is to make the page look more inviting to readers. By breaking a full page of text into a few smaller sections, the paragraphs tell your readers, "Come on, timid reader, it won't be that bad." In this regard, starting a new paragraph whenever you feel like it is not the worst thing in the world. It does make a page look less intimidating, so it fulfills one part of the paragraph's purpose.

However, and more importantly, paragraphs show readers how a long piece of writing is actually a series of smaller units. In your essay, you might explain your main idea with several examples and defend it with several reasons. You can use paragraphs to separate those shorter units from each other so that readers can consider them one at a time. Each example and each reason becomes its own paragraph. Paragraphs do the same work in stories. They divide a large action into smaller steps, and with dialogue, they divide a conversation by its speakers. In reports, paragraphs divide a large set of information into smaller subsets.

To make good use of your paragraphs, you must make decisions rather than guesses about them. You need to understand your essay's main idea. You then need to determine which sets of information or examples are needed to explain your main idea and what information is needed to show readers that it's a good idea. After you decide what to include in your essay, you can then decide how to use paragraphs to present those parts as smaller units of the whole.

To help make these decisions and share them with your readers, you have the topic sentence. You read about this in Chapter 1. The topic sentence summarizes — for you and your readers — the job that a paragraph will perform within a longer piece of writing. The rest of the sentences in the paragraph then show readers what you mean. Those other sentences are called supporting sentences. Below you'll find an example of how a topic sentence (in bold) states what the paragraph will explain. Notice how the supporting sentences then use details to show readers what you mean by your topic sentence:

> **However, and more importantly, paragraphs show readers how a long piece of writing is actually a series of smaller units.** In your essay, you might explain your main idea with several examples and defend it with several reasons. You can use paragraphs to separate those shorter units from each other so that readers can consider them one at a time. Each example and each reason becomes its own paragraph. Paragraphs do the same work in stories. They divide a large action into smaller steps, and with dialogue, they divide a conversation by its speakers. In reports, paragraphs divide a large set of information into smaller subsets.

In this case, the "however, and more importantly" tells readers that one job this paragraph has been given is to respond to the paragraph or paragraphs that precede it. That's a transitional phrase to let readers know that a somewhat different and more important idea is about to be unveiled in comparison to the idea they just read. The rest of the topic sentence then summarizes that somewhat different and more important idea. The supporting sentences explain this idea with information about how it works with essays, stories, dialogue, and reports.

You don't have to use a topic sentence and supporting sentences in every paragraph you write. If readers can figure out what your paragraph is doing without a topic sentence, you can let them. It'll make them feel good about themselves. There are also times when, to draw attention to a particularly important point, you might use a single sentence as an entire paragraph:

Foolish student writers!

You can't get away with that very often. Even a handful of one- or two-sentence paragraphs in a row make an essay strangely difficult to follow. Writing professors call this "choppiness," and rightly so. A string of tiny paragraphs chops the essay into chaotic fragments rather than a neatly divided whole. You can draw attention to an important idea with a short paragraph, but only do that every now and then.

Whether your paragraphs are long or short, and whether they come with topic sentences or not, remember that their primary job is to present one complete part of your main idea and their secondary job is to make the page look more inviting. If you create your paragraphs randomly or by sight, they might only be doing that secondary job. They might then start to wander from your main idea and look for something else to do. You can avoid this by giving each of your paragraphs the meaningful work it craves. Now that you have a general understanding of paragraphs, the rest of this chapter will show you how to use them in your essay.

USING A TOPIC SENTENCE OUTLINE

A topic sentence outline helps you plan the body of your essay by listing the topic sentences for your essay's future paragraphs. You can create a rough draft of a topic sentence outline very easily. All you have to do is make a list of all the possible information you will use to explain your main idea to readers. As long as you have gotten to know your topic properly, you will have plenty of information to share about your idea.

After you make an initial list, you can revise that list by deciding what information to include and how to use it. What pieces of information do you absolutely have to include? What is optional? How many paragraphs should be used to explain each piece of information? What information doesn't really help to explain your main idea, even though it's interesting and related to the topic? By working on your list of information in this way, you can create an outline of the body of your essay.

To build a good outline, you have to think about both parts of the paragraph's job. First, an outline of paragraphs has to show you how the main idea is divided into smaller chunks of information or supporting ideas. Second, it has to make sure that no single paragraph will be too long or too short. Start by planning to write one paragraph for each supporting idea or group of information or example on your list. After that, consider the length of your paragraphs. If they will be too long to be inviting, look for ways to divide them into shorter paragraphs. If you have a lot of short paragraphs that make the essay choppy, look for ways to combine some of them into longer paragraphs.

Planning the Rough Draft Before You Write It

Let's consider how this might play out with an essay of your own. Suppose that your assigned topic was interpersonal relationships. It was probably assigned in a health class. Health classes assign all sorts of topics that you'd rather not think about. Now suppose that the more you got to know your topic, the more you noticed that the seasons have a dramatic effect on interpersonal relationships, especially romantic interpersonal relationships. After rigorous self-reflection, you arrived at this main idea: February is a terrible month for romance.

To explain your idea about February and romance, you have a list of seventeen supporting pieces of information:

1. Flowers are all dead.
2. Birds are gone except for the filthy pigeons that eat garbage all winter.

3. Trees are bare and bleak and depressing.
4. Transportation is an unpleasant challenge for dates.
5. Winter coats are not sexy.
6. Snow pants are not sexy.
7. Rubber boots are not sexy.
8. Runny noses are not sexy.
9. Long underwear is not sexy (usually).
10. There aren't any new romantic comedies in the theater.
11. It's dark by the middle of the afternoon.
12. Seeing people kiss makes me think of germs.
13. The rainy weather makes me want to cry because rain-drops are like tears.
14. I cry all the time.
15. My apartment is too cold to have anyone over.
16. My mother can't figure out how to use a thermostat and calls me constantly to come over and set hers the way she likes it.
17. Who would I call anyway?

That's a lot of information for this idea, and it adds up to a convincing essay. February truly *is* an awful month. However, some of this information is more important than other information. The negative impact of winter coats on romance, for example, is not as compelling as the negative impact of crying all the time. If you give each point its own paragraph, and if each paragraph is about the same length, you'll suggest to your readers that those points are equally important. That gives readers the wrong impression about what matters most.

A more likely problem, however, is that the coat para-graph will be pretty short because it's a bit superficial, while the crying paragraph will be pretty long because there's so much complexity to the many types of crying that you do. If you have too many short paragraphs, the essay becomes choppy. If the long paragraphs get too long, then the essay becomes less inviting. To fix this problem, you combine the shorter, less important points by turning them into supporting sentences for a bigger idea and its paragraph. With an important point whose details would generate an uninvitingly long paragraph, you divide those details into subpoints and give each subpoint its own well-developed paragraph.

Here's what your list of supporting points might look like after some sensible restructuring. Each numbered point now has its own paragraph in the body of your essay. Any lettered points are now supporting sentences within a paragraph:

1. Nature is depressing:
   a. Flowers are all dead.
   b. Birds are gone except for the filthy pigeons that eat garbage.
   c. Trees are bare and bleak and depressing.
2. It's hard to go on dates:
   a. Transportation is difficult.
   b. No new romantic comedies in the theater.
   c. My mother can't figure out how to use a thermostat and calls me constantly to come over and set hers the way she likes it.
   d. Who would I call anyway?
3. Winter clothing is not sexy:
   a. Winter coats make you look fat.
   b. Snow pants make you look fat.
   c. Rubber boots make your feet look stupid.
   d. Long underwear looks stupid except in the right

      lighting and frame of mind.
4. Health concerns impede intimacy:
   a. Runny noses are disgusting.
   b. Seeing people kiss makes me think of germs.
5. The weather is discouraging:
   a. It's dark by the middle of the afternoon.
   b. Rain makes me want to cry because it's so tearlike.
   c. My apartment is too cold to have anyone over.
6. I cry in response to the bad weather.
7. I cry in response to the lack of sunlight.
8. I cry in response to sad, February-related news stories.

With this restructuring of paragraphs, the planned essay does a better job of focusing on the more important information and combining the lesser points so that each of the paragraphs is about as important as the others. It keeps any one paragraph from being too short because of a lack of supporting information. It also divides the crying paragraph into three related points so that each can be a well-developed paragraph instead of a single, uninvitingly long one.

Another benefit of the topic sentence outline is that it helps you decide whether a paragraph belongs in your essay at all. This is more challenging work than you might expect. The more information you look at, the more you have to say. It's shockingly easy to get sidetracked here and include stories and examples and information that have nothing to do with your main idea just because you find them interesting, too.

In this revised outline, for example, you can see more clearly that while all of this information defends the idea that February is a *depressing* month, it doesn't all help to explain the narrower idea that February is a bad month for romance. Is nature, for example, really a necessary part of romance? Do birds have to chirp before you can go to the movies? You might think about cutting that. And bad weather, with the right company, can be great. Haven't you ever heard of snuggling? That's a cheap *and* romantic date. So you might want to cut that paragraph, too.

And while you're rethinking this information, rethink that question about who you would call (2d). A question isn't an idea. If you want to restate that as a piece of information, you need to use the answer to that question, which is that you have no one to call. That's not February's fault, so that shouldn't be part of this essay, either. And the same goes for your mother and her thermostat. She may be annoying, but she's not the reason you're sitting home alone. When you're gathering information, it's sometimes hard to separate good information from bad or irrelevant information, but the topic sentence outline makes it easier to see these distinctions so you can plan a better body for your essay.

You don't have to worry about sticking to one main idea when you're just talking on the phone with an old friend. In that context, you can throw together as many ideas and digressions as you like. Nobody cares. But with the college essay, you're only allowed one main idea. You have to make sure that every paragraph in the body helps you to present that idea to your readers. If a paragraph strays, cut it.

Revising Your Rough Draft After You've Written It

Even though many professors require students to hand in a topic sentence outline with their rough drafts, they're not idiots. They understand that many of my students create the topic sentence outline *after* they write the rough draft. Rather than planning the points to include in their rough drafts, most students look at the paragraphs they just drafted and pull out the topic sentences.

It's hard to stick to one main idea when you plunge ahead into drafting. Once the creative process of drafting begins, your mind has a way of going where it wants to, like a big dog pulling you by its leash down a sidewalk or into traffic. When you don't have an outline to help you stick to your main purpose, it's easy to stray from your main idea. That's why your professor might ask you to create an outline first.

However, if you ignore the thoughtful advice of your professor and draft without an outline, creating a topic sentence outline afterward can still help you clean up any problems in the draft. If no topic sentence exists in a paragraph, for example, an after-the-fact topic sentence outline points out this deficiency. If that paragraph is well made and actually presents one smaller part of the main idea, you can create a topic sentence for it. If the paragraph lacks purpose, you can take a quiet moment to rethink the paragraph as a whole. It might be reshaped to present one small part of the main idea — and then given its own topic sentence — or it might be combined elsewhere, or it might be cut from the essay entirely.

After you make sure your paragraphs are all functional paragraphs, an after-the-fact outline then helps you identify which paragraphs stick to the main idea and which do not. It helps you combine small points into larger ones or divide a large point into smaller subpoints so that the paragraphs are neither choppy nor uninviting. We haven't talked about ways to organize your information yet, but the after-the-fact outline will also help you to organize the paragraphs and correct any paragraphs that stray from your chosen pattern of organization.

An after-the-draft topic sentence outline is thus a good way to revise your rough draft while it's still pliable. You're still better off planning the body of your essay before you write it, but if you find yourself stuck when it comes to creating a before-the-draft outline, it won't be the worst idea in the world to draft the body of the essay first and then come back and revise it with a topic sentence outline. A student writer's gotta do what a student writer's gotta do.

ORGANIZING YOUR PARAGRAPHS

It's possible to write an effective short essay that has no organization other than an opening line, followed by a body of explanation, followed by a closing line. You could write a letter to the editor like that, or an answer on a midterm exam, or an email to a former girlfriend who was offended by the way you playfully kicked her cat. In these cases, you can get away without using organization because the essay is too short to be disorganized. Readers can take in the details and mentally reassemble as your main idea whether or not they're organized.

While you don't need to worry much about organization when your essay is short, you do need to worry about it the rest of the time. Longer papers provide more complex explanations and more detailed information. Without organization, readers have a hard time keeping track of these details and connecting them to your main idea. They forget things. Their minds start to wander. It's like shopping for groceries without a cart. You can only hold so many things in your arms. Organization provides a shopping cart for your readers. The better the organization, the more information they can carry in their brains.

Organization is not a matter of putting "firstly," "secondly," and "thirdly" at the beginning of paragraphs. Instead, it's the careful arrangement of paragraphs to form a larger pattern that readers can then use to organize your essay's information in their minds. Some patterns are built into the topics already, and some you can impose on the information at hand. Either way, the purpose is the same. Organization shows readers how the pieces of your main idea fit together to form a larger idea — your main idea.

To organize the paragraphs of your essay, you have many options to choose from. Internal patterns are a natural part of the information itself, like the chronological pattern within which historical events take place. Logical patterns, such as putting examples in order of importance, emphasize your interpretation of the information. And when nothing else works, you can always build an artificial pattern of your own and use it to hold your information together. That's better than nothing.

USE INTERNAL PATTERNS TO EMPHASIZE THE STRUCTURE OF INFORMATION

The most effective organization tends to be internal patterns — patterns of organization that are already built into a topic or idea or detailed information. They keep the information organized, and they also reveal the natural structure of the information itself. A historical event, for example, is a series of actions and reactions that occur in chronological order. If the topic of your essay is a historical event, you can use the same timeline to organize your own ideas and show readers how those smaller moments that make up the event are naturally structured. A poem is an arrangement of words that usually occur in a linear pattern, moving line by line, word by word, from start to finish. If a poem is your topic, then the natural way to organize your illustration is to follow the poem from start to finish, line by line and word by word. The shape of the poem becomes the shape of your essay.

CHRONOLOGICAL patterns are based on the order in which specific events happened, moving forward or backward. This pattern can be used to present case studies, hypothetical situations, historical events, and predicted future events. *Cause and effect* is a type of chronological pattern that presents either the causes or the consequences of something that happened. You might look at the various causes of an actual or hypothetical event, or at the actual or hypothetical effects of some event, or at both causes and effects. The *problem/solution* pattern is usually chronological, too, because your problem developed in the past, it exists in the present, and you want things to change in the future, first with the solution you propose and then with the effects of that solution.

SPATIAL patterns arrange the details of your information according to the physical location from which the details are taken. These patterns are commonly used with descriptive writing, which tends to describe physical objects and places, but the pattern itself is useful in other situations and in combination with other patterns. You might write about a national crisis, for example, by moving from west to east or south to north with your information. *Visual patterns* are spatial patterns that imitate how a camera lens works, moving from a wide-angle view of a situation to a close-up view or vice versa. If you write about how the price of gas affects the economy, for example, you might start with a wide perspective (the nation), narrow to a smaller perspective (the Northeast), and then to an even smaller perspective (a rural town in Vermont) before broadening back out (the nation).

TEXTUAL patterns are good for essays that ask a question about a particular text, such as a novel, song, film, philosophical essay, and so on. The structure of the text itself serves as an effective pattern for the response. Using this pattern, your essay might follow the order of presentation (Chapter 1, then Chapter 2, then Chapter 3), or it might follow the structure of the thinking (main idea, then main reasons, then supporting information), or it might follow one aspect of a text (the use of a particular word in a poem) as it appears. The key is that you're building an essay that's structured like the text is structured.

ANALYSIS divides the whole topic into its various parts and uses those components as a way to group details together into larger units of explanation and information. These chunks of information are not merely examples of a topic. They are the whole topic divided into its parts. If the topic is a human body, for example, the groupings of information may be the different systems that together make up the whole body — skeletal, circulatory, respiratory, reproductive, and so on. To illustrate the idea that eating an entire bag of marshmallows is unhealthy (even if it does make you feel better momentarily), you might describe the effects of eating that many marshmallows on the various body systems, one system at a time.

Internal patterns are effective because they keep readers focused on the structure of the topic as well as the structure of your thoughts. They remind readers how your topics are (or were) arranged in the real world. These are just a few of your internal pattern options, but it's enough to get you started.

USE LOGICAL PATTERNS TO EMPHASIZE WHAT THE INFORMATION MEANS

Another option is to organize your information with logical patterns that emphasize your interpretation of that information. These work well when there isn't a clear internal pattern to unite the body of the essay. They also work when there *is* a clear internal pattern, but that pattern doesn't really help you present your main idea effectively.

Suppose, for example, that your topic is the best way to prevent body odor. After considering the information, you find there are two effective options — regular bathing and powerful chemicals — and that using powerful chemicals seems to be the better option. To present that main idea, you decide to use an internal problem/solution pattern. You look first at the problem, then at the bathing regularly option, which came first historically, and then at the powerful chemicals option. This gives your entire essay a chronological pattern of organization, and that's fine. However, you can also impose a logical pattern here and put the more effective solution first, regardless of where it fits chronologically, followed by the less effective solution. That works, too, and with a problem/solution essay, it might make more sense.

This organizational choice is no big deal with just two solutions, but suppose you want to compare five solutions for your body-odor problem. Chronological order might then put your best answer somewhere in the middle of the essay. That's a bad place for your favorite solution because the first and last positions tend to be more memorable for readers. In this case, arranging the solutions from most to least effective instead of chronologically makes a big difference. You can emphasize your best answer by moving it to the front of the line. You can then show why the other solutions, one after the other, do not smell as sweet.

LEAST-TO-MOST and MOST-TO-LEAST patterns are useful whenever you want to present reasons or information according to how well they exhibit a particular quality. Any quality will do — effectiveness, cost, size, popularity, morality, importance. Order of importance is popular among student writers, but any quality will do. You then arrange your reasons or examples or sets of information according to how well they display that chosen quality. .

COMPARISON is a pattern to use when your question is about two or more similar items — objects, ideas, people, events, words — and your solution for answering that question is a side-by-side examination. A fairly common type of comparison essay is one that proposes the best solution to a problem. A medical essay, for example, might compare two treatments for the same condition and draw a conclusion about which is the more effective treatment. A literary essay might compare two characters in a novel and draw a conclusion about who made the better decision.

In setting up a framework for the comparison, you have two main patterns to choose from, an *alternating pattern* or a *block pattern.* The alternating pattern looks at one aspect of all the compared items (cost, for example), and then at another aspect of all of the compared items (effectiveness, for example), and so on. The block pattern looks at all of the aspects (cost, effectiveness, etc.) of one item (treatment 1), and then at all of the aspects of the next item (treatment 2).

With both of these comparison patterns, it's a good idea to also arrange your points of comparison according to another pattern — chronological, for example, or most-to-least. That helps readers keep track of them. It's an even better idea to present the details of the comparison in a parallel format. If you look at the cost of deodorants 1, 2, and 3 in that order, then look at the effectiveness of the deodorants in the same order. This helps the readers make a clearer comparison because the details are laid out symmetrically.

USE ARTIFICIAL PATTERNS WHEN NOTHING ELSE WORKS

And then there are times when neither internal nor logical patterns make sense for your information or main idea. Leaving the information disorganized is one option, but it's a bad option. It's better to impose some kind of order than to make your readers put the paragraphs together on their own.

LISTING is one of these artificial patterns. It's better than nothing, but not by a lot. In fact, listing really only makes sense when you have many smaller points to make and can't figure out any internal or logical order for organizing these details. Perhaps you have seven pieces of information to support a proposal, or nine examples of your main idea in action. When that happens, putting your information into a numbered or bulleted list makes the information *look* organized even thought it's not. If you're going to go into management, a bulleted list is the only pattern of organization you will ever need for any of your memos and email, but don't rely on that for the college essay.

A second option is the FAKE INTERNAL pattern. With this strategy, you create an internal-style pattern (time order, spatial, etc.) that isn't really a part of your information and then use that fake pattern as a general framework for the essay. What you're doing is taking something tangible — such as one typical day, traveling from east to west, or a case study — and using that pattern to organize your information. It helps when there's some kind of connection between your information and the pattern you're using, but it's not essential.

The fake internal pattern is better than a random list because it gives the body of the essay an actual structure. Fake internal patterns require some creativity on your part, and for that reason they can be enjoyable to write and satisfying to read. You'll see how that works in the example that follows.

ORGANIZATION IN REAL LIFE

You might recall the topic sentence outline that supported your opinion that February is a terrible month for romance. That outline doesn't seem to offer an internal pattern of information by which you can organize this information for your readers. It remains a collection of more or less supporting points, but those points are arranged randomly.

You could improve that outline by imposing a logical pattern on these points. You might arrange them in a least-to-most pattern. You can use the quality "harmful to romance" and move from least to most harmful. Using that pattern, winter clothing will be a good starting point. That will be okay, but with so many points to make, the power of moving from bad to worse to worst is diminished by the number of supporting pieces of information that you are ranking.

So what about artificial patterns, then? You could list them. That wouldn't be bad. Because you have so many complaints, a list does emphasize that high number. It underscores how many things are wrong with February. A list, however, doesn't weave the information of the body into a unified whole, and that's what you want to offer your readers so that they are more likely to remember the information.

A fake internal pattern seems to be just what you need. Suppose you were to organize the information chronologically according to a typical February day. That's loosely connected to your information about February. It's also tangible for your readers — we are familiar with the general structure of a day. So go ahead and use a typical day as your pattern of organization for this essay. While you're at it, please refocus or delete any of the irrelevant information we talked about earlier.

Here's what you might end up with:

1. Wake up and look outside: Nature doesn't inspire romance.
   a. Flowers are all dead.
   b. Birds are gone except for the filthy pigeons that eat garbage.
   c. Trees are bare and bleak and depressing.
2. Get up and get dressed for work: Winter clothing is not sexy.
   a. Winter coats make you look fat.
   b. Snow pants make you look fat.
   c. Rubber boots make your feet look stupid.
   d. Long underwear looks unattractive except in the right light and frame of mind.
3. On the way home from work: The weather doesn't turn my thoughts toward love.
   a. It's dark by the middle of the afternoon.
   b. Rain makes me want to cry because it's so tearlike.
4. Alone in my apartment in the evening: Dating seems impossible.
   a. Transportation is difficult.
   b. No new romantic comedies in the theater.
   c. Runny noses are disgusting.

d.   Seeing people kiss makes me think of germs.
Lying in bed that night: All I can do is cry. (This is a larger point illustrated by the next three paragraphs.)
5. I cry in response to the bad weather.
6. I cry in response to the lack of sunlight.
7. I cry in response to sad, February-related news stories.

You have the same list of information, with a few deletions, but now it's organized around the framework of a typical day in the middle of the most depressing winter of your life. The information holds together much more effectively than it did a few pages ago, increasing your odds of achieving the purpose of your essay, to give your readers your own main idea (along with the information that gave *you* that same idea).

This will be a depressing and far too personal essay for any college class you'll ever take, so I don't recommend you turn it in. File it away under "Future Projects." You can take some comfort, though, in having learned how to make the paragraphs of the body fit together so neatly. That's something. And you have to believe that March will be better. I'm sure it will be.

CHAPTER 6

EXPLAIN YOUR IDEA WITH DETAILS

Because you've planned the body of your essay, writing the rough draft is no longer a matter of figuring out, paragraph by paragraph, what comes next. Now it's only a matter of sharing, paragraph by paragraph, the information from your topic sentence outline. That's a lot easier, and for most student writers, it's a huge relief from the stress of having to make things up as they go along. Not a few break into song or express their relief with bursts of housecleaning.

Writing the rough draft is still hard work, however, so don't get carried away. You need to explain your idea with sufficient information, and it needs to be detailed information. Whenever you bring that outside information into your essay, you also need to give credit to its source. That's what you'll look at in this chapter. You're still only working on the body of your essay, by the way. Openings and closings will have to wait one more chapter. Sorry.

EXPLAINING YOUR MAIN IDEA PRECISELY

The first thing to do in the body of your essay is to present your main idea as precisely as you can. When you developed your writerly thesis statement for this essay, one thing you did was replace vague terms with more precise ones. Now that you're presenting your main idea to your readers, they need to understand exactly what you mean. So take a paragraph to define the key terms of your essay.

A definition is like a fence. Inside that fence is what you mean by that word. Outside that fence are all the other possibilities. Suppose, for example, that your idea is that fast food is bad food. "Fast food" and "bad food" can mean a lot of different things. Left undefined, they'd require miles of fence to contain all the possible meanings. So if by "fast food" you only mean meals prepared by national hamburger chains — or maybe just one hamburger chain — then you better tell that to your readers so they don't get the wrong idea about what to expect inside your fast-food fence. "Bad food" requires an even larger fence for its possible meanings. So if by "bad food" you only mean "harmful to the workers who prepare it," then put up that tiny little fence around "bad food" so that your readers won't wonder why all the other possible meanings of "bad food" aren't in your essay.

The definition of your idea should match the information you're going to present. If your information about fast food is limited to one national chain of restaurants, then define "fast food" to mean the food from that chain. If your information is all concerned with deep-fried foods, then define "fast food" as "anything cooked in a deep fryer." That's a pretty narrow definition of fast food, but if that's your information, then that's where you need to put your fence. That tells readers that the other definitions of "fast food" won't be part of your essay.

You can also define what's inside the fence of your definition by pointedly stating what's *not* inside the fence. You might suspect, for example, that "fast food" means hamburger chains to a lot of people. If that's not what you mean, then tell your readers to set aside that hamburger-chain definition. Negation can be used anytime, but it's particularly important when your key terms are commonly understood to mean something other than what you have in mind.

Examples also help to clarify your definitions. Whether they're hypothetical, personal, or historical, they show readers what your definition looks like in real life. If you define "fast food" as anything cooked in four minutes or less, you can then offer a list of possible examples — hamburgers, microwave popcorn, corn dogs, deep-fried pickles, and so on — that help readers see just how broad or narrow your definition's boundaries are. Examples are particularly effective when your key terms are abstract. If by "profane" you mean "showing contempt for sacred things," your abstract definition might still be hard for some readers to understand. If you give them an example of what this looks like — spitting on a church, for example — the definition becomes clearer.

Your essay satisfies your readers by living up to the expectations you give them when you first explain your idea. If they know exactly what you mean in the beginning of the body, then they also have a more realistic expectation of what information they should expect in the rest of the body. The more clearly you define your idea, the better chance you have of fulfilling the expectations of your readers.

USING SUMMARIES TO INTRODUCE OR INTERPRET INFORMATION

As you move on to present the detailed information that explains and illustrates your main idea, you'll need to use summaries to tell your readers the meaning of those details. A summary is a statement that compresses a lot of details into a smaller set of words. You can summarize the entire political system of the United States in a single sentence: "The United States is a democratic republic." You can summarize an entire movie — *Casablanca*, for example — with two words: "tediously predictable." The value of a summary is its ability to take a large, unwieldy collection of detailed information and package it into a tidy phrase or sentence that tells readers what those details mean.

For most paragraphs, you should use a topic sentence to summarize the detailed information that's presented by the rest of that paragraph. As the first sentence in a paragraph, a topic sentence tells readers what to expect, and the details in the paragraph then satisfy that expectation. If you end with a topic sentence, it summarizes the meaning of all the details that went before it. If you put a topic sentence in the middle of a paragraph, it's usually to show readers how the details before the topic sentence are related to the details that follow. Wherever you place a topic sentence, the effect on your readers is about the same. It satisfies. They sit back and think, "Nice paragraph. I see what you mean." Careful readers can still figure out the general idea or purpose of a paragraph without the use of a topic sentence, but a good topic sentence will tell them what *you* think the information means, and that's important, too.

A topic sentence tells readers what aspect of the main idea you're going to focus on in that paragraph. If your topic sentence says that *Casablanca* is tediously predictable, for example, you've summarized a single quality about the movie. Readers will now expect the details of that paragraph to explain why the plot of the movie is easy to predict. Just as importantly, it also shows readers that you will *not* be looking at the many other characteristics of the movie. That bit of negation might not look like much at first glance. However, getting into all the complexities of *Casablanca* — the dreary cinematography, the inept casting, the annoying way that Humphrey Bogart sucks on his teeth throughout the movie — could take all night. By using the topic sentence to narrow your focus to one smaller point, you can make the paragraph focus on that one idea with plenty of detailed information and not feel guilty for ignoring the rest of this disastrous movie. Not that you'd actually feel guilty.

Although topic sentences are useful tools, summaries are never sufficient on their own. If you only present a summary and leave out the detailed information, you're telling your readers, "Trust me." Some readers may trust you, but careful readers will not. A careful reader needs to see some or all of the detailed information you are summarizing in order to test the validity of your summary and, to a lesser extent, to measure your abilities as an interpreter of information.

At first glance, this seems kind of mean, doesn't it? "Why can't people just trust me?" you might ask. Well, it's because you're a human, and humans are screw-ups, even when they mean well. They cut corners. They get lazy. They exaggerate. So while it might *look* mean for someone to expect you to back up your summary with detailed information, you could also say that the careful reader is helping you become a better writer — and person, possibly. There's some positive spin for you.

Anyway, my point is that you can't leave your summary standing there on its own without risking the disapproval of careful readers. You should always show the detailed information behind the summary so that readers can see what you mean and then thoughtfully judge whether the summary is accurate.

One other problem with relying on summaries, which is especially important for those of you who begin to whimper and mew when assigned a minimum length for an essay, is that summaries compress acres of detailed information into puny little hedgerows of words. Relying on summaries without including those acres of detailed information will leave you with too little to say. Then you will be faced with the equally unpleasant choices of handing in a too-short paper or repeating yourself until the paper is long enough or inflating your paper with unnecessary words.

Using Detailed Information to Explain Your Idea

To effectively defend a topic sentence and the main idea it supports, you need to rely on detailed information. Details are small pieces of real-world information. They are how things sound, feel, taste, smell, and look. They are the specific prices of items at a grocery store. They are the specific actions — insults shouted, noses bloodied, windows broken — that together become a historical event. They are the actual words of controversial immigration laws, the actual number of killer bees counted by a biologist, the actual weight in pounds of a really good banana split. Even if details are made up — as with hypothetical situations — they must be connected to reality by particulars that your readers *might* see, hear, smell, etc.

Details show readers what your summaries look like in the real world. Their primary work is to establish the objectivity of those summaries and your main idea. However, they also give readers mental images, something that readers can see for themselves with their imaginations. Those mental images are more powerful and interesting than the summaries. Readers love it when their imaginations kick into action. Consider this summarizing sentence: "To keep a relationship healthy, you have to keep it new." That's not terrible as a summary, but left to itself, it's just your opinion, and who are you? To make this idea understood and objective, you have to show readers what you mean with detailed information. That might be the facts recorded in a psychological study. It might be a real-world scenario. Here's an example of how you might do the latter:

> With someone you know very well, such as a long-term girlfriend, you might fall into the trap of thinking that there's nothing new for you to learn about her or for her to learn about you. Instead of asking her about her dreams, you ask her to pass the salt. Instead of sharing your fears and desires with her, you share the Metro section of the paper and maybe half of your bagel. Maybe. Gradually, a relationship that used to be full of surprises becomes full of routines and habits and long hours of watching *Masterpiece Theatre* in silence. It becomes static. It becomes your parents' marriage. But people are always changing — you know that because *you* are always changing — so no matter how well you think you know your long-term girlfriend, you'd be an idiot to think you've learned everything about her. You'd be a bigger idiot to treat the relationship like it was a toaster you paid for a long time ago. To keep a relationship healthy, you have to keep it new.

The details show your readers what you mean by "relationship" and "keep it new." They get the readers' imaginations going, too, because there are particulars here they can visualize. Most importantly, the details demonstrate that such a problem is possible in the real world, that you're not making this up out of thin air. That helps readers take you and what you told them more seriously.

Besides engaging readers' imaginations and helping them to see your idea more clearly, details also help the anxious-about-minimum-length writers overcome their anxiety and lead relatively normal lives. Details expand the essential idea into many particulars. For the length-anxious writer, detailed information means more words, sentences, and paragraphs. It provides the length you need without any unsightly padding or repetition. And if you still run short, you simply add more detailed examples, stories, facts, quotations, and so on. The essay becomes longer, more engaging, and possibly even convincing.

The only unfortunate side effect of giving your readers the detailed information they require is that it takes time to do it right. Putting detailed information into words has a tendency to wear out student writers. After spending long hours assembling precise explanations and paragraph after paragraph of details, student writers often tire of their own writing and start to cut out details for fear of boring their readers.

Understandably weary but still foolish student writers! Yes, after you spend hours and hours working with detailed information, those details may grow dull by familiarity — for you. However, your readers will only spend ten minutes with this same set of details. For your readers, these details aren't boring at all. They show your readers that you've put some thought and research into your essay, that you have a sound basis for your answer to the question. Those details also give your readers something to assemble with their imaginations, and that engages them.

If you don't believe me, try this little science experiment. Write your essay in advance, set it aside for two days, and then read it. I propose that the details that you were sick of two days ago will miraculously become convincing and engaging because the passage of time has changed you from a writer into a reader. On the writerly side of the street, yes, the details can wear you out. Familiarity breeds contempt. On the readerly side of the street, those same details are *great*. So hang in there as you show your readers what you mean. If you get tired, take a break. Go bowling. Shop online for a new toaster, one that will do bagels. Then come back and finish what you started.

It is *possible* to ruin an essay by filling it up with more illustration than your readers need. Readers might not like it, for example, if you add too many detailed illustrations of the same basic idea. It could make them suspect that you think they're dumb. In almost two decades of teaching, however, I've only seen that happen twice, or maybe three times. It's not something for you to worry about, in other words. If you have room for more details, add them.

USING INFORMATION AS ILLUSTRATION AND EVIDENCE

Your first job in explaining your main idea is to illustrate it clearly so that readers understand what you mean. However, because your main idea is also a reasonable *opinion*, you must also explain why you think it's a good idea. For that, you need evidence. Luckily, you found both illustration and evidence while you were educating yourself about your topic.

With information that illustrates, the key quality is that it's detailed. It doesn't even have to be credible information when its job is only to explain and not to defend an idea. You could make up detailed hypothetical situations to illustrate your idea, and these would be as just as effective as actual situations because it's the details that matter. The details are what readers need to see in order to understand how your idea works in the real world.

Information used as evidence has two main qualities. First, like illustration, it should be detailed. That way your readers can judge for themselves what the evidence means. If you use a summary of evidence — that most Americans hate cats, for example — readers have to take your word for it. If you get into the details — in a recent Gallup poll, 341 out of 550 respondents reported that they "hate" cats, and another 86 said they "fundamentally disliked" both cats and kittens — your readers can see for themselves whether your summary is accurate. This is why careful readers trust detailed information more than summarized information.

The second quality that makes detailed illustration effective is objectivity. If an observation is objective, it can be measured or observed in some tangible way. The more objective the information is, the more useful it becomes because you are showing your readers that the information is true in the real world, apart from individual perceptions and gut feelings.

This doesn't mean that there is no spiritual reality or that your emotions aren't important. It doesn't mean that the many intangible elements in our lives — such as regret, for example, or a deep-rooted fear of clowns — are insignificant. Reliance upon objective information simply reflects our status as three-dimensional creatures. Those three dimensions are the common ground we share with other humans. Information that exists in three dimensions (numbers of salmon, words in a book, sworn courtroom testimony, and so on) can be observed or measured by anyone and thus becomes more reliable than information that is intangible or internal.

You have many types of information to use in the body of your essay. Some are more useful for illustrating your main idea, and some are more valuable for defending your main idea. What follows is a quick review of common types of information and their range of usefulness as illustration or evidence.

PERSONAL EXPERIENCE

The only reason I'm alive today is because I wasn't wearing a seat belt. If I had stayed in the car when it rolled, I would have been crushed to death.

Personal experience is usually a good way to engage your readers' imaginations because readers like stories. When it's detailed, a personal experience works well to illustrate an idea. However, personal experience is rarely effective when used as evidence because its scope is limited to you and because we can so easily misunderstand our own experiences. Careful readers are rightly suspicious when personal experience is the basis for an entire essay. The example above is engaging enough as an opening illustration, but it would only serve as evidence for a very narrow idea ("seat belts don't *always* save lives").

PERSONAL OBSERVATION

Some people smoke a couple packs of cigarettes a day and still live to a ripe old age. My great-aunt Marjorie was a chain-smoker and lived to be 94. She never had health problems in all her years, and she would still be alive today if not for an unfortunate chainsaw accident.

Like personal experience, personal observation is useful primarily as a type of illustration that connects well with your readers. As evidence, it usually won't prove much of anything because we are rarely able to observe more than a narrow set of information and because we lack the training to judge the significance of that information.

REFERENCE INFORMATION

Aristotle was a Greek philosopher. His writings create a comprehensive system of Western philosophy, including treatises on the topics of morality, aesthetics, logic, science, politics, cats, and metaphysics.

Except in the case of defining key terms, the information you find in reference works probably won't and shouldn't find a home in your essay. Reference works summarize broad bands of information so that you can get to know a topic quickly. They often point you toward more detailed sources of information, but they rarely give you those details directly. Because it's not detailed, the information from reference works won't be very effective as illustration or evidence. These reference works are still important, but the information you find there is useful to you primarily when you are getting to know your topic, not when you are presenting an idea to others.

PROFESSIONAL OPINION OR OBSERVATION

Chief Dye of the Chickawack Fire Department says that squirrels are second only to cigarettes as the source of home fires. According to Dye, squirrels chew the electrical wiring in attics, electrocuting themselves and bursting into dangerous, squirrel-shaped flames.

Professional observation is more useful information than personal observation because the professional draws upon a broader range of training and experience than the average person. Even without scientific training, the first-hand experience and continuing education of the professional leads to more credible observations and judgment. As long as a professional observation includes detailed information, it will serve as good illustration. It will often be convincing evidence, too.

The key to using this information as evidence is making sure your professional is qualified to make observations about that subject. If the professional strays from her or his area of expertise, the value of that opinion quickly diminishes. That's like when an actor in a commercial tells you, "I'm not a doctor, but I play one on TV" — and then prescribes a pill for you. In the same way, a preacher's ideas about politics or a professional basketball player's ideas about religion shouldn't be taking more seriously than anyone else's personal observations and opinions.

How the professional comes across to the readers is also important. If the professional sounds like a jerk or a bozo, readers won't like the person, and the professional opinions, even if they are valid, will then be less valuable as evidence. Even careful readers can in this way be just as shallow as anyone else.

SERIOUS POPULAR INFORMATION

Bolivia has had 126 governments in 125 years of existence. More than 100 of these governments have been established by military coups like the one that took place last Tuesday when the leader of the Bolivian Navy took control of the government and immediately announced plans to attack Chile to gain access to the Pacific Ocean.

Serious popular information comes from newspapers, reference books, textbooks, magazines, and websites that are written for an educated but general audience. In some cases, these sources are written by scholars in the language of normal, non-nerdy people. In other cases, they is the work of professional writers who either find the information directly (usually with news and current issues) or who translate the work of scholars into the language of normal, non-nerdy people.

The information from these sources is usually great for illustration because it makes complex ideas easier for normal people like your readers to understand. It's also useful as evidence when the topic is a news item or current issue. With those current topics, newspapers and magazines and news websites tend to provide the most reliable information.

For topics other than current events, however, you usually need to dig deeper into the topic to see if your serious popular information is accurate. With popular magazine and website articles, that means looking at the details of scholarly information to see if the professional writers have presented those ideas accurately. After you've done that, you don't really need the information from the magazine or website. You can use the more credible scholarly information instead.

Scholarly Information

The five-legged male Agalychnis callidryas *in Group A were 38% less likely to produce tremulations during breeding rituals than were the four-legged male* Agalychnis callidryas *of Group B. However, the attraction of four-legged females to the males of Group A was 13% higher than to the males of Group B. This suggests that Jabin (1997) may be correct in her theory that the five-legged* Agalychnis callidryas *don't need tremulation because the mutation itself attracts breeding partners who are curious to see what it's like to be with a five-legged mate.*

Scientific information is gathered and analyzed by people who, like other professionals, work with a certain body of knowledge but who have also been trained in standardized methods for developing and testing information and ideas. This training creates a level of quality control. Working within a scientific discipline also means that these professionals must publish their findings to their peers for review and testing. The publication process provides another layer of quality control because academic peers will gladly cut each other's throats over the slightest mistake.

There is still plenty of room for faulty, incomplete, or manipulated scientific information. Some scientists have made up study results to secure future grants and impress their friends. It also happens that a rogue government will sometimes edit the science in its agencies' reports for the sake of political goals. In the end, however, the scientific systems come with safeguards that clean up and remove that kind of junk — eventually.

Besides being more credible, scholarly information is usually more detailed than other sources of information. Scholars have to show their work to their peers, and that means showing them the detailed information upon which their ideas are founded. Those objective details — and the credible interpretations of scholars — are both good types of evidence to use in your own essay.

The one thing that scholarly information doesn't do well is illustrate ideas. Scholarly work is written in the professional language of full-time, professional scholars, people who are so deeply immersed in their disciplines that they rarely see the sun, much less speak in the language of normal people. Unless your audience is made up of full-time, professional scholars, you'll need to decode the scholarly information for the illustrations to make any sense. For most audiences, similar information from serious popular sources will be more effective as illustration.

Textual Information

In Amy Tan's The Joy Luck Club, *Waverly feared her mother's opinion of Rich. He was "not only not Chinese," he was also younger than Waverly, and somewhat short. She feared her mother would point out Rich's flaws one at a time, "each one flung out like a piece of sand, one from this direction, another from behind, more and more, until his looks, his character, his soul would have eroded away."*

When your topic is a text — a story, poem, play, essay, and so on — the best illustration and evidence you can bring to your essay will be information from the text itself. You might also be able to use historical information or scholarly opinion about the text, but even that is used primarily to explain the meaning of the textual information. It's best to rely on the text itself as the main source of your evidence. The more detailed that information is, the more effective it becomes as evidence because it shows readers that your ideas really are based on the text itself.

Giving Credit to Your Sources of Information

Academic honesty and professional courtesy require that whenever you use ideas or information from sources outside your own experience or observation, you must tell your readers where the information came from. That includes actual words, ideas, stories, information, descriptions — *anything.*

If you don't give credit to your sources, you're guilty of plagiarism. Unfortunately, "plagiarism" is just another vague English-teacher term for most student writers. It sounds like a mild medical condition, a foot rash or inflammation of the elbow. You got plagiarism? No big deal. Put some ice on it. Take an aspirin.

That's why I prefer to use a different word for plagiarism. I call it *stealing*. If you don't give credit to the sources of your information and ideas, you are a thief. You're taking the credit that belongs to another writer and giving it to yourself. Do you remember how you felt about the person who broke into your 1986 Honda Civic and stole the car stereo that was worth more than the car itself? That's how you should feel about yourself when you don't give credit to others. It shouldn't feel okay.

The first step in giving credit to your sources is the decision to give credit to your sources. This is a choice you have to make. For that, you're on your own, just you and your conscience. If you and your conscience decide not to do this, however, then you and your conscience might soon be assisted by the Dean of Students and his or her conscience. Even if you feel okay about it, stealing words and ideas remains a serious offense at college, as the Dean of Students will explain.

The second step is learning how to give credit to others. There's a lot of popular misinformation and plain old folklore out there about when you do or do not need to give credit to others, so do your best to get forget of any ideas you already have about how this works. They are probably wrong. Instead, pay close attention to the guidelines that follow — and then follow them, of course.

GIVE CREDIT EVEN WHEN YOU PARAPHRASE OR SUMMARIZE

Contrary to popular belief, you can't just "put it into your own words" and call it good. Putting someone else's ideas or information into your own words doesn't make those ideas something you thought of that information something you gathered. It only obscures who actually deserves credit for the ideas. Whenever you use someone else's ideas or information in your essay — whether you quote them directly or rephrase them — you must tell your readers who did the work.

One way to do this correctly is to *not* paraphrase. Instead, make a direct, obvious connection between the source of the borrowed words and the actual words you are borrowing. That looks like this:

> In a recent letter to the *Itemizer-Herald*, Bill Florence writes, "You people need to stop looking down your noses at Food Mart dining. At my gas station, the corn dogs are never more than three days old, and the burritos are updated *daily.*"

> Regarding the use of torture at the community college, Chickawack Community College's Assistant to the Associate Dean of Instruction, Dr. Robert LeRoy, Ed.D., said that a boring lecture couldn't be considered torture because it "induces rather than deprives a student of sleep."

In these examples, there's no question about which words belong to you and which belong to your outside source. It may seem a little cumbersome to do this properly, but that's okay. It's a little cumbersome to do almost anything properly, especially when other people are involved. At some point, you have to either accept that cumbersomeness is a part of life or find yourself eating a lot of microwaved dinners with a cat.

You can still paraphrase the ideas and information you find, of course. In fact, that's what you *should* do with most of that information, using direct quotations only when the original source is particularly important or states something exceptionally well. The difference between honest and dishonest paraphrasing is how you give credit to its source. You must be just as direct and obvious as it is with a direct quotation:

> According to Bill Florence's letter to the *Itemizer-Herald*, the corn dogs at the Texaco Food Mart are always less than four days old and the burritos are always less than two days old.

> Chickawack Community College's Assistant to the Associate Dean of Instruction, Dr. Robert LeRoy, Ed.D., denies that boring lectures are torture because there's no sleep deprivation involved.

GIVE CREDIT PRECISELY

Just as paraphrasing is not a legitimate way to avoid giving credit whenever credit is due, it's also not sufficient to introduce your source and then let your readers guess which information came from the source and which came from you. You need to give credit *wherever* credit is due, too. That means clearly connecting specific sources to the specific ideas or information that you've borrowed.

"Are you kidding me?" ask many student writers.

"No," I tell them, "I'm not kidding. I do not kid."

"But I used, like, four sources in one paragraph," they complain, often with pained expressions to underscore their deep intellectual anguish.

"In that case," I tell them, "you need to give credit where credit is due, like, four times, sentence by sentence." It looks like this:

> Another threat to sea lions is their increasing addiction to marijuana. In the journal *Science*, J. Ballard provides evidence that bundles of marijuana jettisoned by smugglers have become a favorite meal for sea lions. The *San Diego Union-Tribune* reported that the annual number of reports of stoned sea lions has risen five-fold over the past ten years. This may seem harmless enough, a victimless crime, but a recent study by the Oregon Department of Fish and Wildlife suggests just the opposite. The increasing number of sea lions with "the munchies" has been connected to depleted steelhead runs, the harassment of heavily armed fishing fleets, and the consumption of poisonous three-legged starfish, which according to ranger Jill Rupert, "kind of look like Doritos." All of this puts sea lions at a much greater risk of extinction.

Yes, that *is* a bit cumbersome. It takes some getting used to. That's okay, anguished student writer. It's better than stealing from those sources. If most but not all of the information in a paragraph comes from a single outside source, you must clearly distinguish which material comes from you and which does not. This also means moving through your paragraph sentence by sentence to show your readers who gets credit for what. You don't need to introduce the single source multiple times, but you do need to refer to it as needed:

> This past November, the *Kansas City Star* reported that beef simply does not taste as good as it used to. According to their exposé, "The Beef with Beef," reporter Van Stavern found that beef, once the king of meats, now regularly loses in taste tests to pork, chicken, and halibut. Stavern also found it mattered little whether the beef in question was cubed, ground, or jerked. This seems hard to believe, but when given this same test, my football-playing, gun-toting brothers all agreed that they preferred a lightly marinated chicken leg to a delicious cheeseburger. This raised an important question for me: Is the quality of the meat changing, or are our tastes changing? The *Star* exposé doesn't answer that question, but this essay will.

Another common error in handling outside ideas or information occurs when students refer vaguely to "studies" as the source of information without identifying the titles of the alleged studies or the names of the alleged researchers. Sometimes the studies are obviously made up by dishonest student writers who suppose that writing professors won't be able to recognize fake information. Little do they know, we sometimes can. More often, however, this vagueness comes from basically honest student writers who can remember the information but not the website where they found it. They hope "studies" will be sufficient.

Basically honest but foolish student writers! When this failure of memory occurs — and it occurs all the time — you're faced with three options. One is to use the information, as you remember it, without giving any credit to its forgotten source. This is the easiest thing to do, but it's also lazy and unprofessional. And it's *plagiarism* — the bleeding ulcer of academic disorders! Stealing! So that's out. The second option is to *not* use the sourceless information. That's ethical, so that's good, but it also weakens your essay. A third option is to go back to the computer or library and track down the actual source of the information so you can give it proper credit. This is the best way to solve this problem, even though it takes time and self-discipline. Even better, of course, would be to avoid the problem altogether by taking better notes as you educate yourself about your topic.

One final error to mention is that student writers will sometimes feel quite satisfied with putting quotation marks around borrowed words, like this:

> Many people think she's a hair fanatic. "Her hair makes you think she's hiding drugs in there, or perhaps a small animal. It's beyond big." It might be wrong to judge someone by how she does her hair, but hair is an important part of the impression a person gives.

The quotation marks are a start because they tell readers that these exact words came from someone other than yourself, but if you don't provide the specific source of those words, the original author hasn't received the credit that's due. It's also distracting. Your readers stop reading your paragraph and start wondering who the author is and where you found the quotation. It's better to name the source directly, like this:

Many people think she's a hair fanatic. In a recent *New Yorker* article, fashion critic Syd Darby writes, "Her hair makes you think she's hiding drugs in there, or perhaps a small animal. It's beyond big." It might be wrong to judge someone by how she does her hair, but hair is an important part of the impression a person gives.

GIVE CREDIT WHEN YOU INTRODUCE INFORMATION

You should give credit to a source before you offer its information. If you present the information to readers and follow that with a statement of where it came from, you've given credit where credit is due, but you've also given your readers an unnecessary second or two of confusion. Consider these two examples:

Used coffee grounds contain traces of ammonia and tannic acid and should never be eaten, even as part of a nationally advertised diet plan. That's according to the Surgeon General.

According to the Surgeon General, used coffee grounds contain traces of ammonia and tannic acid and should never be eaten, even as part of a nationally advertised diet plan.

Both examples say where the borrowed information came from, but the second does so without puzzling the readers at any point. Formal documentation systems often allow you to cite your sources immediately after you use their information, so that's fine. However, even with formal documentation, your essay will tend to be more readable if you use the name of the author to introduce that information.

WITH LESS FORMAL WORK, GIVE CREDIT WITH ATTRIBUTION

In all of the examples above, you see something that writing professors call "attribution." This is a somewhat informal way to give credit to your sources by mentioning a few key pieces of information — often the author, title, and publication — in the body of the essay. Those pieces of information connect your quotation or idea or bit of information to a specific source. They also provide your readers with enough information to allow them to find that source for themselves in case they want to learn more or find out if you are being honest.

Attribution is a common practice in journalism, where it lives within a fairly complex set of guidelines and standards that we won't get into here. For a journalist, it's sometimes okay to attribute information vaguely ("according to high-level sources") in order to protect the source of that information from retribution. However, even for journalists, it's only okay to be vague like this when you really do have actual sources to protect. You almost certainly don't have any high-level sources to quote — yet — so your attribution must always be more precise than that.

Attribution is a good starting point for giving credit to your sources, so it's often used with short essays, reflection papers, and informal assignments. In addition to the principles you've just read about, effective attribution also requires you to know how to punctuate direct and indirect quotations. If you don't know how to do that, you should invest 45 minutes relearning the rules for quotation marks.

Punctuation guidelines aren't a part of this book, but they're not hard to find. If you're reading this book as part of a class, you might already own a grammar and punctuation handbook. If so, look up "quotation marks" in the index. If not, ask your professor to recommend a good, cheap handbook. Many professors have a stack of sample handbooks in their offices and will eagerly *give* you one to encourage your unexpected and gratifying interest in punctuation. You can also go to your computer, type "quotation marks" into any Internet search engine, and then work your way through the first five or six listings that have ".edu" in the web address. You'll find what you need.

With Formal Work, Give Credit with Formal Documentation

The further you go in your education, the more likely you are to use a system of formal documentation to give credit where credit is due. Most likely, you've run into formal documentation before now. Writers in the humanities — including your writing professors — tend to use and promote a documentation system developed by the Modern Language Association (MLA). The MLA system requires you to mention the author and page number whenever you use information in your essay, like this:

In *Call Me Herman*, Melville writes that *Moby-Dick* was never meant to be taken seriously (231).

Moby-Dick was not intended as a philosophical treatise in the form of a whaling novel but "a bunch of hilarious hijinks, just for laughs" (Slemenda 301).

At the end of the essay or term paper, the MLA system asks you to provide a full set of bibliographic information. Here's what works cited entries look like:

Melville, Herman. *Call Me Herman: The Official Autobiography.* Boston: Owl, 1842.

Slemenda, Steve. "Is Melville to be Trusted?" *Journal of Whaling Studies* 39 (2003): 295-308.

This list of works cited in your paper makes it possible for the reader to find and read your sources. The last name and page number you give readers in the body of your paper sends them to the correct listing on the works cited page. They can then use that information to find the source and read it for themselves.

There are several documentation systems out there. Many writers in the social sciences use a system developed by the American Psychological Association (APA). This system requires you to cite the author and date of publication when you use information from a source. The rest of the source information goes into a bibliography at the end of the essay. Other disciplines use a similar system developed at the University of Chicago. Some science papers put a numbered list of sources at the end of the paper and then cite just the corresponding source number within the body. The documentation system you choose will be the one that's most appropriate for the discipline in which you're writing. It will also be the one your professor tells you to use.

All these systems have two things in common. First, they all cite sources briefly in the body of the paper and provide full bibliographic information elsewhere — footnotes, endnotes, a bibliography page. Second, the details about how to do this are shockingly complex. There's a different way to cite every slightly different type of source — books with one author, books with two authors, books in translation, websites, interviews, newspaper articles, journal articles, articles retrieved from a database, articles cited within a book by Peruvian flute players. To make matters worse, those rules change every two or three years when the scholars in charge of these systems get together to collectively change their minds.

Don't get me wrong. Formal documentation is a good thing. It provides a common set of rules for all students and scholars within a group of disciplines. You can all give credit when and where credit is due in the same way. This allows everyone to concentrate on the ideas at hand. Even so, learning how to use formal documentation can still be a nightmare.

When it's your turn to learn how to use formal documentation, take a deep breath and then find a good reference guide. For all of these systems, one option is to buy the guidebook that's published by a particular scholarly organization. Most college handbooks also come with abbreviated versions of the guides that are still sufficient. And you can find what you need online for free at many academic websites, such as Purdue University's Online Writing Lab.

What you *shouldn't* do is try to memorize all those rules. That's too much. You'll start having dreams about punctuation and indentation, which is just weird, even for English majors. Just find a guide you like, and then practice using it. That's all you need to do.

CHAPTER 7
GUIDE YOUR
READERS

After you've put some time into drafting the body of your essay, the essay can become so familiar that you don't actually see what you've written. For you, the essay exists both as ideas in your brain and as words on the page. When you look at what you've written, you see an essay that makes perfect sense. You see how your information defends your main idea. You see how the paragraphs fit together. And if anything *is* missing on the page, your brain fills in that missing piece so that you won't feel bad about screwing up. Your brain loves you.

Your readers, on the other hand, having no direct access to your brain, only see the words that actually made it onto the page. If you left any gaps in your explanations, even small ones, your readers stumble. And even if you presented all the information clearly, your readers still won't be as familiar with your idea and information as you are. From their perspective, the main idea might be hard to figure out. Your information, even if it is organized, might appear disorganized or disconnected from a main idea.

Your readers aren't stupid. They just have other things on their minds — dishes to wash, toilets to repair, carbohydrates to avoid — so they could use a little help when it comes to following your essay. Even your writing professors, who are usually the best readers you'll ever run into, have lives of their own outside the classroom. Most of them, anyway. They might try to patiently unravel your peculiar thought processes and make sense of an incomplete or too-subtle essay, but you can't count on it. So if you want to be understood, you have to treat your readers as if they are a *little* stupid — like people talking on cell phones while they drive. Assume that you don't have their full attention.

You need to give your readers far more guidance than you think they need because — this is important — they are not you. For them, this is the first and probably only time they will see your essay. So make your main idea unavoidably clear in the opening. Point out the organization in the body with fairly obvious transitions. Okay, you tell them, here comes the second of my four examples. Okay, now you get the *third* of my four examples. When it's time to wrap things up, you have to give your readers a closing that reminds them about the information they just read. Go ahead and mention all the main points of the body, too, because there's a good chance they've already forgotten those points. Then remind them, one more time, how the essay works together to explain and defend your main idea.

And yes, we finally come to the long-neglected opening and closing of the essay. You may have wondered why they have been neglected for most of the book. It's because they don't matter that much. The body of your essay does the work of explaining your main idea to your readers. The opening and closing are just accessories to help your readers understand what's going on in the body. They are important, but their importance is secondary and measured by how well they help readers understand the body of the essay.

This chapter offers several techniques to help you guide your readers. It looks at how topic sentences and transitions can show readers how the smaller parts of the essay fit together. It shows you how the opening will help your readers see the purpose of your essay and how the closing will make your main idea unavoidably clear and perhaps even relevant to their lives. As long as *you* know how your own essay works — what the main idea is, how the information is organized — these techniques will help you to make your essay much more effective.

USING TOPIC SENTENCES AND TRANSITIONS

If you've made a topic sentence outline of your essay, then you understand the different ways in which your paragraphs serve the main idea as examples, reasons, and groups of information. If you have organized your essay, then you also understand how your paragraphs are arranged according to patterns within the body of your essay. The best way to guide your readers through your essay is to share this understanding with them, to show them exactly how your paragraphs fit together. You can do this with a few simple tools that we'll look at in a minute.

However, there is a slight chance that you are still just cranking out essays without planning them. Old habits die hard, especially when they worked so well for you with simpler papers in simpler times. If you haven't outlined the body of your essay, and if you haven't consciously organized your paragraphs according to a pattern, then you don't really understand how your essay is structured. Because you don't have an understanding to share with your readers, you're going to be a lousy guide.

You have two options. The easy option is to ignore this chapter and hope that your subconscious mind was brilliant enough to save you from disaster. The better option is to study the essay that you've cranked out and outline it so that you begin to understand its structure. Then, if it's not organized or if the structure is incomplete in some way, revise the body of the essay so that it is organized and complete. You will then have the understanding you need to guide your readers through the body of your essay. What makes this option better is that it builds your writerly skills and gives you more conscious control over what you write. That will help you to use writing more effectively to accomplish many tasks, not just writing essays.

Use Topic Sentences to Connect Paragraphs

The most direct way to guide your readers through the body of the essay is with topic sentences. You've seen how they tell readers what to expect from a paragraph. That's part of guiding readers. You can also use topic sentences to show readers how paragraphs connect to your main idea. Suppose, for example, that the main idea of your essay is that gasoline taxes should be raised to pay for solar power development, and suppose this is the current topic sentence for a paragraph:

> Generating solar energy will remain expensive using current technology.

That's fine, but you can expand the information in the topic sentence so that it also tells readers how the paragraph connects to your main idea. If this paragraph explains a reason to raise taxes, you could use this topic sentence:

> Gasoline taxes need to be raised to support solar development in part because generating solar energy will remain expensive using current technology.

This sentence shows readers what information will be inside the paragraph (the cost of current technology) and that this is a reason for the main idea (taxes need to be raised to support development). If the paragraph is related to the main idea by providing some reassurance for doubters of that main idea, you could use this topic sentence:

> These taxes don't have to be permanent because generating solar energy will only be expensive using current technology.

You can also use a topic sentence to show the relationship of one paragraph to another, or to show how a paragraph fits into a larger organizational pattern. Suppose you have a paragraph that presents details about the danger of cigars to one's health. You can use your topic sentence to connect that paragraph to others with references to those others or with transitional words or phrases. Here are two examples:

> Pipes are okay if you want to die, but cigars are great.

> Cigars are far less dangerous than cigarettes, and they're less dangerous than chewing tobacco, too, but they will still do their best to kill you.

In both cases, the topic sentence now connects this paragraph to prior paragraphs. In the first example, the topic sentence refers backward to a section about pipes. In the second example, the topic sentence refers backward to two prior sections about cigarettes and chewing tobacco. It also shows you that the pattern being used is one of decreasing danger.

To make your topic sentences more useful, you should start by making sure that your paragraphs have topic sentences to begin with. You may find, to your horror, that some of your paragraphs are missing topic sentences. "What the — ?" you will say. Don't finish that sentence, horrified student writer. Instead, read the offending paragraph closely. Does it have a purpose? If so, add a topic sentence now. That shouldn't be too difficult. If the paragraph doesn't have a discernible purpose, then you need to think about this. Does it need to be edited so that it rejoins the other paragraphs in presenting your main idea? Does it need to be removed? Do what you have to do. If the paragraph still has a place in your essay, give it a good topic sentence.

Once your paragraphs are properly outfitted with topic sentences, you can expand and rephrase those topic sentences so that they connect directly to your main idea or other paragraphs. Don't be bashful about this. Your readers need you to be obvious. That's what kindness looks like in this situation. It's fine to flat-out announce that this paragraph is an example of the main idea or that this next paragraph will present the most compelling reason to accept your idea.

If you lack the courage or good manners to be so blunt, then at least add short phrases to your topic sentences to show how the paragraph is part of a larger idea. You can add phrases that refer backward to past paragraphs — "more importantly," "another example," "a bigger mistake." You can add phrases that look forward to future paragraphs — "before we look at the results," "the first of the three examples," "in the early stages." You can repeat important words or phrases from your main idea to remind your readers about that idea. Do *something*. Your topic sentences long to live more fulfilling lives in your essay — certainly you can understand that — and this is how you give them that fulfillment.

USE TRANSITIONS TO POINT OUT RELATIONSHIPS AND ORGANIZATION

Transitions — whether they are sentences, phrases, or individual words — help readers see how the parts of your essay fit together. They might point out the relationship of two or three items, as in a list, or they might point out the organization of the whole essay.

Transitional statements are usually single sentences found at the beginning and end of subsections of the essay. They might be topic sentences, or they might act like topic sentences for multi-paragraph sections of the essay. At any pivotal point, you can also use a transitional paragraph to explain how the writing that follows is related to the writing that went before it. Here's a transitional statement that's also a topic sentence:

> Before one can understand the full effects of addiction to high-fructose corn syrup, it is important to first understand the chemical makeup of this seemingly benign substance.

This transition does two things. The first half prepares your readers for a broader set of paragraphs that examine the full effects of this addiction. That tells them what they can expect in the coming paragraphs. The second half introduces the chemical analysis of high-fructose corn syrup and suggests that it's not so benign. That tells them to expect some detailed information about this point in the paragraph.

Here are examples of transitional statements that might show up later in this particular essay:

> So much for the chemical makeup — what about the effects of these chemicals on the user?

> Dehydration is only the first and least consequential effect, but even more troubling is the rapid rise in heart rate.

> As if these effects weren't bad enough, high-fructose corn syrup also leads to dangerous levels of hyperactivity that turn the "syrup-sucker" into a human whirligig.

> The worst effect, however, is the drawn-out depression that follows the abuse of high-fructose corn syrup, a depression that grows deeper and more difficult to escape with each round of syrup-sucking.

> With effects this severe, why are kids today turning from traditional recreational drugs to high-fructose corn syrup?

These statements might seem a little obvious when pulled out of paragraphs and listed like this. They are. They should be. As your essay gets longer and gives readers more to think about, obvious statements like these become less obvious and more helpful. Collectively, this group of transitions helps readers see both a cause and effect pattern and a least-to-most harmful pattern within the body of the essay. The repetition of the key term "syrup-sucking" reminds readers, again and again, that this is the topic of the essay. That's exactly what your distracted readers need in order to fit together the pieces of your essay.

Transitional phrases and words work like transitional statements, but they do so within sentences instead of standing on their own as independent sentences or paragraphs. They are easy and effective additions to topic sentences, and you can use them within your paragraphs. Some transitional phrases show how ideas are logically related to each other as additions or examples or contrasting thoughts. Here's an example of how transitions (in bold) work within a paragraph:

> **When you finally come to the end of your excuses,** the only option left is to look at your mistake **and then** admit that you blew it. My mother calls this "the point of no return." **When you finally arrive at the point of no return,** you're

not only willing to admit your mistake **but also** to abandon it. **For example**, you admit that **in the past** you were petty about splitting expenses exactly down the middle. You shouldn't have asked her to pay for half of a beer from which she only took a sip. That was dumb. **In the future**, you won't do that. You will **instead** be generous. You **also** admit that **in the past** you were maybe a little harsh in your comments about her appearance. You didn't need to ask if she was retaining water or just putting on weight. That was dumb **and** mean. **In the future**, you won't make those comments, even if you're seriously wondering. **In the future**, you'll be kind. **When you finally get to the point of no return**, it may be too late to save a relationship, **but** you can at least move forward toward a healthier future **by** not repeating those kinds of stupid mistakes.

These shorter transitions refer either to the pattern of organization for the essay ("even worse," "in the past," "in the future") or link two ideas with a word or two of transition or sequence ("however," "for example," "but," "not only"). The repetition of key terms also helps us to remember the topic and purpose of this paragraph.

Transitional words and phrases don't stand out as much as full transitional sentences, but they still do a good job of helping your readers see how smaller pieces of explanation fit together. You should use them *a lot*. Even when they seem to draw attention to themselves — as with all the "in the future" and "in the past" repetition — they are actually drawing attention to the organization (before and after) and the main point (change over time), making it more likely that your reader will see this. It's hard to overdo it with transitions.

USING AN ENGAGING YET OBVIOUS OPENING

Once the body of your essay is complete, it's time to write the opening and closing — finally. You remember the openings from your old friend, the five-paragraph trainer-essay. For that opening, you used some kind of catchy hook to introduce the topic ("According to Webster, a 'catastrophe' is 'something that is catastrophic.' That certainly describes my recent trip to Iowa."), and you followed it with your thesis statement ("Never vacation in Iowa because of the heat, the humidity, and the profuse sweating."). Would you be surprised if I told you this kind of opening is no longer sufficient?

With almost any kind of writing, the opening has two jobs. First, it should engage your readers' interest. Second, it must show readers what to expect. With the college essay, engaging your readers' interest is a little trickier to understand. On the one hand, your readers are probably the professors who assigned your essays, so they will read them whether or not you engage their interest. You just don't want to set up barriers for them with *dis*engaging openings like the one above. On the other hand, you'll share some of your essays with other students, and they will read more carefully if you engage their interest with a good opening. With both types of potential readers, however, the main job for the opening is to clearly let them know what to expect.

Here are a few standard opening techniques that you can use to engage your readers and show them what to expect.

THE BIG PICTURE

Readers usually enjoy seeing the big picture before you zoom in to present a narrower question and your main idea. Providing some context shows your readers that your topic is part of something larger, and that you're aware of this. It acknowledges the limitations of your essay, too, which is a good thing. It shows readers that you're only going to concentrate on one part of the big picture — and that you're doing this intentionally, not accidentally. Here's an example:

> The two-party political system has been a part of the American scene since before there was a true sense of what "the American scene" was. It hasn't always been Republicans and Democrats, of course, but it has always been two main parties. Whenever a third party has arisen for one reason or another — the Bull Moose Party of Teddy Roosevelt's time or the Republican Party of the mid-1800s — the third party either gained enough power to displace one of the previous major parties or it faded away to become one more footnote in American history. With so many problems present in our current political mess, it's no wonder that reform parties are making headway in their efforts to enter this political system. However, the question remains whether or not today's minor parties will survive more than a few years.

In this opening, the author discusses the bigger picture of two-party politics in America and then zooms in to look at one part of this topic, whether a modern third party could make it in the American political system. If you have an interest in politics, or perhaps if you're surprised to learn that there weren't always Republicans, this might get your brain curious about why this is so.

You'll notice that you don't get a readerly thesis statement with this opening. A readerly thesis statement is not the monster sentence you wrote when you were defining and improving your main idea. That was your *writerly* thesis statement. The readerly thesis statement is a streamlined sentence that captures the main idea briefly and, let us hope, elegantly. You don't find one in this opening, but the opening still works because readers don't need to know the main idea yet. They only need to know what the topic is and what sort of main idea they can expect.

ANECDOTES

An anecdote is a brief story that uses a personal experience, hypothetical situation, historical incident, or other event to introduce your topic. This is popular because stories are easy to remember and they show how an idea works in the real world. Whether you use real-life anecdotes or invented ones makes little difference to your readers. Stories are stories. You can also start with just half of an anecdote and save the other half for your closing. Here's an example of an opening anecdote:

> When I was twenty-two, I shot myself. It happened while I was cleaning out my uncle's trailer. He'd been using the drawer of his bedside table for an ashtray, and when I dumped the cigarette butts into the garbage can, I found that he'd also been using it as a gun locker. His handgun went off when it landed in the garbage can, and the bullet passed through my calf and out through the wall.

> I was lucky, but many others aren't. Thousands of family members die every year because of these weapons. Don't get me wrong about handguns. In spite of what happened to me, I remain ready to defend the right of every American to own handguns. But these handguns should come with one simple safety feature that will keep them from putting family members at risk: removable triggers.

In this two-paragraph opening, the first paragraph tells the anecdote, and the second paragraph transitions from that anecdote to an introduction of the topic and main idea. Spending so much time engaging the readers makes this more informal than most academic essays need to be, and some fussy professors might complain about that. Even so, those same fussy professors might not realize yet how tired they are of colorless, to-the-point openings. An opening like this might thus be quite effective. You just have to be careful about whether it's appropriate for a particular audience.

This opening does include a readerly thesis statement. It's the last sentence of the second paragraph. This sentence doesn't capture the full complexity of the essay's idea — that's the job of the *writerly* thesis statement — but it does briefly state the main point that the rest of the essay will explain and defend.

TEXTUAL REFERENCES AND QUOTATIONS

When your topic is a text of any sort, good manners and professional courtesy require you to introduce the author and title of the text early in your opening, like this:

In Willa Cather's *My Ántonia*, the narrator . . .

Besides this obligatory introduction of the general topic, your text, you will also do well to focus your readers' attention on some relevant quotation or illustration from the text itself that will show readers what to expect from your essay. Here's an example:

> In Willa Cather's *My Ántonia*, the narrator, Jim Burden, makes a big deal about every little thing he remembers. Looking back on his childhood experience of arriving on the Nebraska frontier in the middle of a moonless night, he writes: "There was nothing but land: not a country at all, but the material out of which countries are made. . . . Between that earth and that sky I felt erased, blotted out. I did not say my prayers that night: here, I felt, what would be would be." It's understandable that this would be a bold memory for a young boy to carry, but would that boy be wrestling with the big questions of existence while on that wagon ride or would he simply be trying to keep from falling out of the wagon? That leads us to another and more important question: Just how far can we trust this narrator?

This sort of an essay might not be your cup of tea. In fact, you might need a strong cup of coffee if you're not a fan of American literature. However, you can see that the opening does a good job of introducing the topic — the narrator of Willa Cather's novel — and that it uses this passage to introduce an important question about his reliability. You don't get a thesis statement, but you still know what to expect from the essay. The main idea will be an answer to that question.

Textual references aren't limited to essays about texts. They can be used with any topic. You might use them to illustrate an idea in the same way you would use an anecdote:

> When Huck Finn finally gets some money at the end of Mark Twain's novel, *Huckleberry Finn*, he is able to handle civilization for about a month and then says it's time to "light out for the territories." He disappears from view, never to be seen again. During the last decade, thousands have followed Huck Finn in his flight to the territories. These are young professionals who have amassed small fortunes in a few short years as stockbrokers, software engineers, and baristas. Suddenly they realize they find no pleasure in material gain, and they slip away to Oregon, Alaska, or New Zealand, never to be seen again. They are looking for something else, something just beyond their grasp. But here's a little secret: They won't ever find that elusive something else in "the territories." Huck Finn never found it. Nobody does.

In this example, the quotation introduces the topic of "lighting out for the territories." The author then shows how this continues in current times and presents the main idea of the essay — that neither financial success nor escape to "the territories" is the "something else" that so many of us are looking for. The reference to *Huckleberry Finn* is only here to get us started. This will not be an essay about Twain's novel.

PROVOCATIVE STATEMENTS

Another way to engage your readers is to lead off with a line that seems untrue or that stirs up emotions for your readers. These provocative statements jolt readers' brains into action. As long as you follow up with thoughtful discussion and appropriate information (and thus bring the readers around to your way of seeing things), this is an effective technique for openings.

Here is an example of a provocative opening:

> Abortion is *not* murder. A fetus has no legal status as a human and thus cannot be murdered any more than a brain tumor can be murdered. Those who argue otherwise are wasting everyone's time, including their own.

This one gets the blood pumping whether you think you will agree and want to read the essay to test your own ideas or you think you will disagree and want to read the essay so you can tear this idea apart. As long as this paragraph isn't simply baiting the audience — that is, stirring them up emotionally without delivering a thoughtful idea — something like this can be either an effective opening or the effective first half of a two-part opening.

Here's another provocative statement:

> It doesn't take a penis to be a man.

Okay, so what *does* it take to be a man? If you wonder how this author will define manhood, and if you aren't turned off by the use of the word "penis," then this is an effective first line of an opening. You should be warned, however, that any sort of reference to body parts, sexuality, bathroom functions, and what may be considered off-color language by your audience is risky business. Using shocking words merely to shock readers is a bad policy, and it's been done so much that it's become a bit of a cliché, too. It almost always gets your readers' attention, but it's often the last thing that an offended reader sees before putting down the essay.

Here's an opening designed to frighten the reader:

> Chewing gum seems harmless enough, but every year it strangles more than a thousand children. Once it is lodged in the throat, chewing gum becomes almost impossible to remove with any technique. Death is slow, terrifying, and made unbearable by the ironic minty freshness.

Scary statements are usually effective, too. Again, it's rude and ineffective to bait readers, but if you have information to back up the statement, stirring up a little fear is a good way to draw readers into the essay. In most cases, if you start with a wild or scary statement, the essay will need to show why that statement makes sense — and perhaps isn't as wild or scary as it seemed at first.

OTHER TECHNIQUES

In addition to these common techniques, you have a couple of other options that don't usually stand on their own as openings but may still be useful when used with other strategies.

HUMOR is not common in academic writing because academics are generally humorless. That means you won't get away with much of it. However, a *little* humor slipped in quietly can make an opening more engaging for readers, even if they don't quite understand why. That was good, thinks your biology instructor, not realizing that what she likes about your opening is the way you introduce the topic of frog eggs by explaining how they have the texture and *taste* of Gummi bears. In academic writing, a little humor goes a long way. Anything more than that doesn't go anywhere.

QUESTIONS are another useful device. If you ask a question that readers are curious about, it engages their curiosity. Just make sure you eventually answer any questions you raise — even if your answer is that this particular question has no easy answer. There's nothing worse than asking a great question and then denying your readers the satisfaction of a great response. That's like asking a friend, "You remember that twenty bucks I borrowed?" and then adding, "I still don't have it. Ha ha." It's not good for the relationship.

ARE YOU SURE I DON'T NEED A THESIS STATEMENT?

Yes. Trust me. I'm a professional.

The old rule that you must have a thesis statement in the first paragraph is, like the five-paragraph trainer-essay that required it, too simple for more sophisticated essays. With some essays, the opening will be more effective if you include a thesis statement and then let the rest of the essay defend that idea. With others essays, the opening will be more effective if it raises a question for your readers. The body of the essay can then show your readers how your information leads to a convincing answer. You have to decide what works best, essay by essay.

Technical papers, scholarly research, and some scientific papers require an opening that includes a statement of what the essay will cover. That's because they are written for readers who are eager to read these papers but only if they contain the information or ideas they are looking for. Those science people hate to waste time.

Unless you are bound by an academic discipline's formal restrictions, or unless a professor tells you to use one, it's your choice about whether or not to put a thesis statement in the opening. Your readers need to know what the topic and purpose of the essay will be. They need to know what sort of idea to expect. However, they don't need to have that main idea spelled out for them in the first paragraph. It can wait until the end of the essay.

USING A TRIUMPHANT CLOSING

One good thing about writing the body first and the opening and closing later is that you might actually write a closing. When student writers start with the opening and then write the body, they often wear out by the end of the body. Having said all they really need to say in the body, they scribble down the barest of closings and quit. They become long-distance runners who sit down with ten yards to go and tell the cheering fans,

"You get the point. I more or less ran the entire race."

Foolish student writers! Are you tired? Take a nap. Then come back and tell your readers about the triumph that is the body of your essay. Remind them of your main points of information. Remind them about how those points work together to explain and defend your idea. But don't stop there. You should also give your readers something new as a parting gift — one final and engaging illustration that captures your main idea, or perhaps a few practical suggestions for what your readers can do with your idea.

Although you're right to think that the body of a good essay has said everything that needs to be said, your distracted readers need more than that. Detailed information presents your idea clearly and effectively, but reading a lot of detailed information all at once can be overwhelming for a reader. To guide your readers through to the end of your essay, your closing has to summarize that information and briefly remind readers how it all adds up to explain your main idea. The closing should also emphasize that idea one last time.

The closing doesn't have to be long. It just has to be complete. Here's a single closing that's only a paragraph long but still wraps things up effectively:

> Who then should bear the blame for this catastrophe? The evidence is clear enough. Delvin Baird hired the uncertified electrician who installed the overhead lava lamps. Delvin Baird never scheduled the electrical inspection that would have shown that the overhead lava lamps were defective and dangerous. Delvin Baird removed the sprinkler system without any mention of this to his clients, even though he met

> with them 14 times after this decision. Only one person is to blame for what happened on November 21: Delvin Baird.

The repetition of the villain's devilish name is the only writerly device the author uses here. It reminds us of the topic of the essay. Otherwise, this is a simple summary of the main points of information from the body followed by an equally simple restatement of the main idea. That's long enough. It does its job.

If you want to wrap things up more colorfully, that's fine, too, as long as you still do the more important work of summarizing your information and emphasizing your main idea. You have many options for adding color to your closings, just as you have many options for openings. Anecdotes are popular. You can also bring in textual references and quotations. In addition to these favorites, you might try two other techniques that are only used with closings — the second half of an anecdote and the call to action.

THE SECOND HALF OF AN ANECDOTE

You set up this technique by telling the first half of an anecdote in the opening of your essay. That gives your readers some motivation to continue reading — to find out how the story ends. At the end of the essay, you reward them with the second half of the opening anecdote. Here is an example:

> What happened to Wild Bob? Unfortunately, Wild Bob's story ended like that of many others who suffer from TF. He lost his job because of the safety risks he posed. His family

was driven away. Finally he gave up, sealed the air vents in his room, and let the disease run its course. Wild Bob's story illustrates how desperate life can be for victims of TF.

As you've seen, however, ongoing research suggests that relief is on the way. Friesen and Friesen's identification of the "TF gene" is a step toward long-term eradication. Dr. Libby's research with monkeys builds on their efforts, opening the door to the gene therapy proposed by Dylan in her ground-breaking paper. In the short term, the Beeler Foundation's "smelling nose" cats offer immediate help, as does the Cooper brothers' creative use of water filtration technology. And let's not forget Richardson's astonishing results with therapeutic bowling, suggesting that a solution might be found with simple lifestyle changes.

As this and other promising medical research suggests, we can soon write a new ending for the TF story. For that to happen, the research must move forward. This is why Congress must renew its funding for the TF Institute. The results of current work are too promising to be ignored. For all the Wild Bobs out there, continued funding is a matter of life and death.

This closing starts by giving readers some resolution with the sad ending of the Wild Bob anecdote. It follows that with a thorough summary of the information from the body. The last paragraph then connects both Wild Bob and the summarized information to the main idea — keep the money coming because the research is making progress. This is probably a little long for a short essay. You don't want the closing to overshadow the body. However, it's just right for a longer paper that has presented a lot of detailed information.

THE CALL TO ACTION

The call to action builds a bridge between the main idea and your readers by giving them practical ways to make the main idea a part of their lives. If a call to action is appropriate for your main idea, it comes with several advantages. Each action you call for is an application of your main idea to real-life situations. More importantly, it makes your idea tangible for your readers. If they see how your idea connects to their lives, they understand it more clearly. The only weakness is that, on its own, a call to action doesn't summarize the details in the body and connect them to the main idea. That's easy to fix, though. You summarize the information first and then call your readers to action. Here's an example:

> Unfortunately, ending the practice of clear-cutting is more easily said than done. The majority of private forests are now held by huge timber corporations, and short-term profit is their primary goal. The majority of public forests are managed by government agencies that see our forests as agricultural crops. These factors make it challenging for the average person to influence forest practices directly. However, there are three easy, effective things to do to indirectly reduce or even remove clear-cutting as a widespread forest-management practice:
>
> 1. Use less timber. Buy recycled wood products such as OSB sheeting, HardiPlank siding, and decking made from plastic and recycled wood. These alternatives are becoming more common and can be found at most building supply stores.
>
> 2. Make your priorities known to your current elected representatives with letters and email. They won't know you're

unhappy unless you tell them, and they are savvy enough to know when the tide has finally turned.

    3. Vote for politicians who care more about ecological forests than corporate profits. They are out there, and in increasing numbers.

    We can make a difference. We just have to take some first steps and encourage others to join us in doing the same. The rest will follow.

This is a lengthy closing, too, and again, that's okay as long as the body of the essay also takes its time laying out the details of its information. In this example, you have a writer who knows that the body of the essay is solid and is now taking a little victory lap.

Good for you, triumphant student writer!

Chapter 8

Proofread Your

Essay

After you have written an essay for a class, you might be tempted to turn it in. Don't. It's not time yet. You have one more important task in front of you.

"No way," you tell yourself. You feel good about this essay. It really flowed, and now you're ready to hand it in.

Don't. The sense of accomplishment you feel is well earned. It's not easy to bring something new into the world, so it's kind of a big deal for you to know a topic well enough to figure out an idea of your own, and it's also a big deal that you have taken that idea of yours and figured out how to explain it in an essay. That was a lot of work, a lot of personal investment of your time and intelligence. You *should* feel a sense of accomplishment when you write the last line of your triumphant closing.

However, that sense of accomplishment is merely personal. It's you feeling good about what *you've* done, not about what your essay's done. You don't really know what your essay's done yet because you haven't read it carefully yet. When it comes to assessing the effectiveness of your essay, all that matters is what's on the page. To judge whether your essay is really any good, you have to set aside your personal feelings and judge your essay the way that your readers will judge it — by actually reading it and testing whether the words on the page do their job.

Most student writers refuse to proofread their own essays after they've finished writing them. Can you believe that? I bet you can because the odds are that you are one of those students. If that's the case, then you need to take yourself more seriously as a writer, and that means taking your readers more seriously. They are going to judge you by what you hand over to them. Don't give them any reason to disregard your intelligence because of stupid little mistakes in your essay. Make sure that the words on the page are as good as the ideas they are trying to explain.

In this final chapter, we'll look at how to proofread your essay before you turn it in. You will have to ignore any feelings of accomplishment — or sense of dread. You will also have to give yourself enough room at the end of the writing process so that you have time to proofread. The main thing, though, is that you have to *decide* to proofread.

HOW PROOFREADING WORKS

Proofreading is the process of examining your own essay from the perspective of a fairly picky and unimpressed reader. You then use that fussy perspective to look for mistakes and other distractions in your essay so that you can remove them and thus make your essay more effective for your actual readers. It's not a matter of simply reading your own essay before turning it in. You have to mentally step away from your essay and read it as if you hadn't written it.

Proofreading focuses mostly on the surface of the essay — word choice, sentence grammar, punctuation, formatting, and so on. That's because by this point in the writing process, the essay as a whole should be pretty good, with no major revision required because of weaknesses in information, organization, logic, and so on. That's probably how it is with your essay as long as you properly educated yourself about your topic, developed a good idea, planned out your essay, explained your idea in detail, and guided your readers through the body of the essay. If you *haven't* written a pretty good essay, proofreading won't do any damage, but it also won't miraculously transform your lousy essay into a good one. For that, you'll need Chapters 3 through 7. Keep that in mind for your next essay.

One reason student writers tend to avoid proofreading is that it's kind of discouraging. You're trying to find all the mistakes you made, which has a way of pointing out that you sure made a lot of mistakes. This is why so many student writers turn to their friends and loved ones when it's time to proofread. They want *en*couragement rather than *dis*couragement, so they hand off their essays to readers who will find the good in their work and praise them for it.

That's understandable, but it's not a very effective way to get better at something. If you want to improve your skills, you need to work on your weaknesses, not just affirm your strengths. It's the same story with learning to write essays. You have to suck it up, student writer, and look for the mistakes and bad habits. Facing those weaknesses is the best way to turn them into strengths.

The most difficult and most important requirement for effective proofreading is distance — intellectual distance. You really do have to look at your essay as if you hadn't written it. You have to look at it as if you are a reader who doesn't even know you, who doesn't know how hard you've worked on this or how good you feel about it. You have to get to the point where your essay is just a collection of words on the page that might have been written by anyone so that you can judge how well those words are doing their job.

It's almost impossible to do this very well. Even professional writers, people whose livelihood depends on the effective use of words, have a hard time separating themselves from the things they have written. However, there are a number of practices and resources available that will help make the proofreading process more successful. And the more proofreading you do, the easier that process will become. It also helps to know what exactly to look for as you're proofreading. The rest of the chapter will focus on just that.

EXAMINING YOUR WORDS CAREFULLY

Even if you have educated yourself about your topic and used your new understanding of the topic to develop an insightful idea, it's easy enough to drive your readers away from that idea with unwise word choice. My sister Nadine, for example, once told my mother to "get the hell out" of her bedroom. In the weeks of punishment that followed, it was discovered that Nadine had presented my mother with a reasonable idea. Nadine had been preening in front of the mirror in her underwear when Mom barged in to ask where the vacuum cleaner was. Nadine, then in the bloom of her prolonged adolescence, made an understandable request for privacy. That idea might have been taken seriously, too, if she had chosen her words more carefully. As it was, her word choice made her audience blind to her idea.

Student writers, one would hope, are not likely to swear at their readers, but that doesn't mean that they can't undo a lot of otherwise good work by choosing their words without care. Consider this paragraph:

> Nowadays it sucks to be a student because there's never any way to make it happen without taking out TONS of student loans. My dad got GRANTS to go to school back in the day, free money, money he didn't even NEED, really, and his parents gave him money, too. Going to school now means basically taking out a mortgage on my LIFE. Is that fair? No way!

If we look just at the observation and the short bit of information offered, this is a reasonable opinion. For this student, going to school requires many dollars in student loans. Compared to the public support that was available to the student's father, the student is in a far worse situation. However, that's not what you notice about this paragraph. You notice the CAPITAL LETTERS and conversational tone and the word "sucks." This approach is not uncommon for student writers. Wanting to connect with readers, they work hard to *not* show off their intelligence with smarty-pants techniques such as precise language and grammatical sentences. Instead, they simplify their complex ideas into a friendly, vague, conversational style.

Foolish student writers! That's not how you connect with your readers. Your readers don't want to be your friend. They want to understand your idea. That means you need to address your readers precisely, intelligently, and respectfully. If you have a good idea — and I'm confident you do — then translate that idea into exact, formal language and assume that your reader is up to the task of understanding it. Don't try to be friends with your fussy readers. That will only make them reject you — and probably your idea, too.

Besides adopting a more serious tone, you should also avoid inflammatory words. Swear words, for example, are almost never appropriate in the college essay. Vulgarity rarely works. You know that, though. A more common mistake is to present your ideas with words that make fun of topics or ideas that are important to your readers. In doing that, you make fun of your readers, too. Consider these three topic sentences for the same paragraph:

Senate Bill 211 could have the unintended consequence of
raising the infant mortality rate in our state.

Senate Bill 211 is a threat to children.

Senate Bill 211 is ridiculous.

Now imagine that you support Senate Bill 211.

In the first topic sentence, the writer states an idea that you
should take seriously but doesn't put you on the defensive. This
is only a *possibility* to consider. The writer assumes that it would
be an unintended consequence, not a malicious act by its spon-
sors. As a supporter, this sentence is still challenging for you.
You may not want to hear this. However, because the writer
brings it up respectfully and objectively, you are more likely to
read the paragraph that follows with an open mind. The writer
has earned enough credibility for that.

The second topic sentence is less precise, so you're not sure
what to expect from the paragraph, but the real barrier is the
word "threat." Senate Bill 211 might indeed be a threat, so
the idea might be accurate, but that word suggests intentional
harm, and that could make you feel defensive about the bill,
even though you don't know yet what the writer means by this
word. The vagueness gives the impression that the whole bill
is a threat, too, so that's more reason to continue with a much
less open mind. The writer has made the job of convincing you
more difficult by using this provocative word. It lowers your
confidence in the objectivity of the writer.

The third topic sentence is insulting, and you as a supporter know that the real-world information about this bill

doesn't support that kind of disrespect. The bill isn't worthy of ridicule. It's thoughtful work. It might not be perfect, but it wasn't written by baboons. When you see a vague and insulting topic sentence like that, it almost doesn't matter what follows. The writer has shown contempt for something you support, and that's contempt you might easily feel on a personal level. If you read the paragraph at all, you will read it with distrust for this writer.

So if you as a writer have taken the time to build a good essay, take a little more time to choose your words carefully. Presenting your idea with appropriate, precise, respectful language helps you to connect with your readers. Sloppy or offensive language creates an unnecessary barrier between you and them.

How do you examine your choice of words to make sure that they are appropriate, precise, and respectful? I'm sorry to report that is one of the hardest things to do as a proofreader, and it requires outside help. Most student writers are sadly inadequate judges of their own word choice. They need some help from people who are better with words than they are. The more time you spend proofreading, the more you become familiar with your bad habits, and this will help you to avoid them and become more careful with your words as you move forward. But that only happens with a prolonged effort. In the meantime, get some help.

The most effective way to learn how to look at your word choice from the eyes of a careful and somewhat fussy reader is to ask a careful and somewhat fussy reader to read your essay and examine your use of words. Your professor is just such a reader, and you can benefit from his or her perspective on your essay. However, your professor's comments will probably come to you after the essay is turned in rather than beforehand, as a part of the proofreading process. Even so, getting some graded comments afterwards will help you on the next essay you write, so pay thankful attention to that feedback and, if you have any questions about those comments, ask your professor. Better yet, make your professor earn his or her probably inadequate salary by making an appointment to go over your essay after you get it back. I know that might feel like going to the dentist when you don't have to, but there's a lot of value in getting that informed perspective.

If you're enrolled at a school that has a writing center, you can find fussy readers there, and they can be used to help you gain a better perspective on word choice as part of your proof-reading. You can bring those writing tutors your assignment instructions and complete essay and simply ask them to help you with word choice. These are people who are into words, so sometimes they get a little nerdy, but if you pay attention and ask them to explain any comments you don't understand, you'll soon begin to see your work through their eyes. This is one of the most efficient ways to give yourself an informed, readerly perspective on your own writing. Just don't get defensive about it. Remember that you asked them to show you the problems with your essay.

If you don't have access to a writing center, you might have access to others who have at least some background with academic writing. These might be relatives who were English majors before they got into food service. They might be friends who have done well in writing classes — or who are just hard to please. As long as these readers are willing to be honest about what's confusing or distracting with the words you've chosen, they can help you to separate yourself from your own writing and see it through your readers' eyes. But be careful about using friends and relatives. Don't get mad if they tell you there are problems. When you do that, you end up missing the problems and losing them as future readers. Thank them, instead. Buy them pizza or babysit their kids. You need to honor their efforts to help you with your word choice because careful reading is not the easiest thing to do.

When you're writing an essay for a class, you also have access to other students who are writing essays for that class. In some cases, your professor will require you to share your work with those students, to offer and receive feedback. When that happens, make the best use of the opportunity by making your essay as good as you possibly can before you share it with others. That way, anything useful you hear from other students will be something you didn't already figure out on your own. It will help you to make the essay better than you could have made it by yourself. Second, pay attention to what they say. Keep your mouth shut and listen. Your colleagues might not be able to explain themselves very well — they are still just students, after all — but they can still identify the words in your essay that were confusing, and that will help you to take another look at those same words.

If your professor doesn't require you to share drafts with others, you can still seek out others in the class and ask them if they'd like to form a proofreading group. You probably won't do that because of how nerdy that sounds, but it's still a good idea. Math people don't have any trouble looking for help from among their own colleagues. They form study groups without a second thought, like it's a normal part of the learning process. I don't tend to look at math people as role models, but in this one case I think they have the right idea. Working with others really does help you to step outside of your own intellectual barriers and see things from a broader perspective.

REMOVING DISTRACTIONS

Formatting, sentence structure, spelling, and punctuation are the most superficial components of a college essay. Your ideas and explanations are what matter most, but these components form the actual physical product that readers hold in their hands and read. They are what your readers use to understand your idea and explanation. Any errors with these superficial elements become distractions for readers. The more you distract your readers in this way, the harder it becomes for them to pay attention to — or even notice — your ideas and explanations.

Another thing to keep in mind is that first impressions do matter. If your essay looks good on the surface, some readers will see that and assume that the thinking must be good, too. Many others will take you more seriously when they see you know your way around a sentence or that you're an old pro with the formatting requirements of formal documentation. On the other hand, if your essay doesn't follow required format guidelines, some cranky professors might not even read it. The impression you give has a way of making the rest of the essay more or less effective.

FOLLOW FORMATTING AND ASSIGNMENT GUIDELINES

You should be thoughtful about the format of your essay. If the assignment requires formal documentation, it also requires the formatting rules for that documentation system, which includes margins, page numbering, allowable font sizes, and more. These rules are detailed and thorough, but it's nothing you can't handle. You just follow the documentation guide that you can find in a writing handbook or online.

If the assignment requires no formal documentation, it's still a good idea to follow the formatting rules of a documentation system. That extra effort makes you look like a more serious student, even if you're not, and it makes your essay more readable. If you set your carefully formatted essay down next to the handwritten essay of another student, you'll see what I mean. So will the other student. So will your professor.

Your professor will often add other rules beyond formatting. You might need to stay within minimum and maximum length requirements. You might need to use a minimum number of sources. Don't think of these rules as suggested guidelines. Think of them as felonies you'd rather not commit. Ignoring those guidelines tells your professor that you've decided to not take the assignment seriously. When you do that, your professor is not likely to take your work seriously, either. This is a kind of proofreading that you can do on your own, but don't rely on memory when you do it. Reread the assignment instructions. It will take two minutes.

Formatting might be a little trickier, especially for the first couple of essays, and especially if you don't know how to use your word-processing software. However, you have many resources to help you with that, too. Any recent writing handbook will give you explanations and examples of how to format a paper. If you have access to a writing center, the tutors there have been formatting papers almost since birth and will find great pleasure in helping you with yours. The Internet is also filled with templates you can use, guides for formatting a paper with your particular software, and other help. Just use the obvious key words to search for those resources.

WRITE GOOD SENTENCES

The most serious distractions in college writing are sentence-level mistakes with grammar, punctuation, word usage, and spelling that college writers are expected to avoid. I understand, grammatically challenged student writer, that all of these technicalities were taught when you were in fifth grade, and that the only thing you remember from fifth grade is the afternoon your sister Nadine busted you for smoking cigarettes in the attic with Mike Stradley and Steve Rayner. I understand how totally unfair it is that now, after all those misspent years, you are expected to write proper sentences.

Unfortunately, that gross unfairness doesn't change anything. You are now responsible for your sentences, and that's

just the way it goes. If you have any problems writing grammatical sentences, as you almost certainly do, it's time for you
to work on these technical skills so that your readers will be
able to see your excellent ideas instead of your faulty sentence
structure. This might take some work, but it's rewarding work.
It builds confidence. And if you've been doing any reading at
all since fifth grade, you'll be pleased to find out that your technical skills are better than you think.

Proofreading for sentence-level errors can be difficult work
because of the technical expertise that it requires. However,
even if your sentence-making skills need improvement, you
can still proofread your work to make sure each sentence makes
sense on its own. The problem that gets in the way of that is
your brain. Your brain knows what's supposed to be on the
page, so that's what your lying eyes will probably see when they
proofread, whether or not it's really there.

To overcome your brain, you need some practical methods for creating that intellectual distance you read about at the
beginning of this chapter. One method is to let time create
that distance. Finish the essay a day or two before the deadline
and set it aside. Then come back to the essay and see what
you think. You'll be amazed. It won't be the same essay. Your
brain will have moved on to other tasks, so if you left out the
word "not," you'll notice that now. Similarly, if you misspelled
a word or used "comma" instead of "coma," you'll probably see
that now and fix it.

If you don't have a day or two to let the essay cool off, you
can also ask someone to read your paper to you. That puts
you in the place of the audience by turning your essay into a

spoken thing that exists entirely outside of your brain. This also helps you identify sentences that don't make sense. Whenever your reader stumbles, stop the reader and fix the sentence. If you have no one around who is willing to read your essay to you, read it out loud to yourself. That's not as effective, but it's better than reading it silently. When you read it out loud, it's harder for your brain to trick you into thinking that everything's fantastic.

If you know that you have trouble with ungrammatical sentences, then even before you have learned all the rules for writing good sentences, you can read your essay backward, sentence by sentence, making sure each sentence makes sense as a complete thought. That's one test for grammatical sentences. This is also a good way to identify sentence fragments that sometimes make sense when their meaning depends on a prior sentence. Like this one. You will still need to work on your technical understanding of how sentences work, but reading your essay backward will at least help you to identify problems.

What you really need, for the long term, is to develop better technical skills. You need to go back to fifth grade and reclaim the laws of grammar and spelling. Because you have read so many grammatical sentences since fifth grade, your brain has been able to develop a pretty good sense of how sentences and punctuation work. At this point, you probably only need to work on four or five things to write your own grammatical sentences consistently. However, you will need to work on four of five things from a list of a hundred possibilities.

For that reason, it's a good idea to get some help identifying the grammatical guidelines that you need to work on. If you have a writing professor, and if your writing professor has not already told you what to work on, ask your writing professor what to work on. If you don't have a writing professor but attend a school with the good sense to fund a writing center, use that excellent resource. There you will find people who can get red-faced and teary arguing about the correct use of commas in lists. That's the kind of misplaced passion to avoid in your own life, but it's great as a resource when you need to improve your sentences.

You can also develop better technical skills on your own. You can use an Internet search engine to search for information about comma rules. That's a good starting point. How did I know you needed to work on comma rules? Because *everyone* needs to work on comma rules. Everyone was taught to put a comma wherever you would take a breath, and that is one of the worst rules of thumb ever. Commas are related to the meaning of your sentence, not the size of your lungs. Learn to follow comma rules and you'll fix at least one of your problems. You can also find a used grammar handbook and start reading through it, a few pages at a time. This won't be fun, but those handbooks do cover everything, so reading one will refresh your memories of fifth grade — minus the cigarette incident — and help you relearn rules of usage and punctuation.

I can also tell you one thing to *not* do. Do not trust software to fix your spelling and grammar errors. That's just asking for trouble. Spelling errors are bad, but spell-checking errors are worse. A spell-checking error occurs when your software tells you that you've misspelled a word — which is fine — and then suggests a correctly spelled word to replace it. This is where the trouble occurs. If you don't look up the meaning of that suggested word, you might easily accept a very distracting suggestion. Spell-checkers are also blind to your own correctly spelled but incorrectly used words — such as "ill" when you need "I'll" or "sea" when you need "see" or "sew it goats" when you need "so it goes."

A colleague once showed me one painfully funny example of a spell-checking error. The student meant to write this: "I tried to insinuate myself into the conversation." The student misspelled "insinuate," however, and then blindly accepted the advice of his software. The sentence became this: "I tried to inseminate myself into the conversation." That must have been embarrassing, student writer.

Spell-checking errors are great fun for writing professors. They send them around to everyone in the department and yuk it up at your expense. But these errors also ruin otherwise good essays by distracting readers so powerfully. So go ahead and use the spell-checker to find misspellings, but also use a dictionary to look up the meanings of your alternatives before you accept them.

Grammar-checking software is even worse, by the way. The last time anyone actually needed to use a semicolon was June of 1908, so turn down any semicolon suggestions. Turn down any grammar-related suggestions. Turn that feature off, in fact. If you can't tell the difference between a sentence that makes sense and one that doesn't, software isn't going to solve the problem.

You instead need a few points of theory and some individualized help to recognize how those grammatical theories work in your own writing. So go to your writing professor, or your college writing center, or a good thick handbook of grammar to get started. It's not that complicated, but you do need to understand actual ideas about grammar. You need to stop guessing.

KEEPING PROOFREADING IN ITS PLACE

One last thing to remember about proofreading is that it should be the last thing you do with your essay before you print it on clean white paper and put a staple through the upper left corner. You've worked from the inside out to build this essay, starting with your main idea and then adding the body paragraphs that explain your idea. From there, you worked on the opening and closing. You added transitions and improved your topic sentences. That was a lot of work, but now that work is done.

As a proofreader, you're not rewriting the essay anymore. At this point, you're only trying to make a good thing better. You're brushing the teeth of your essay to freshen its breath and to remove any parsley that got stuck in its smile. This is important work because you want to make a good impression and because you don't want any distractions to get in the way of your essay's success. However, it's still superficial work. You're winding down, so don't get wound up about all the other paragraphs you could have written for this essay. This probably won't be the last essay you ever write.

If proofreading leads you to the chilling realization that what you've written is not, in fact, a good or appropriate essay for an assignment, don't panic or despair. This is just an essay, after all. It has its place in the universe, but it's not a very big place. What matters more is what you do with this chilling realization. You need to see it for what it is — a sure sign that you could have done better. Go ahead and turn in that essay, such as it is, and then, when you write your next essay, do better.

Conclusion

The Real Meaning
of "Essay"

There's one final thing you should know about the college essay. The word "essay" means, in so many words, "to fart around." Go ahead and look it up. The dictionary editors are too embarrassed to use that actual phrase in their dictionary, but it's implied. This is something they don't teach you in high school for obvious reasons. It's something they don't teach you in college because college is such a serious place. Even so, it's true, and I'll prove it to you.

Let's go back to your professors and the reason they assign essays in the first place. They don't assign essays for their own benefit. They don't even assign them because they care about you personally — they barely know you. No, they only assign essays — at no small personal cost to themselves — because they want you to enjoy their disciplines the way they do. Writing an essay is your chance to play at being a professor.

And what do professors do when they're not teaching? They fart around! They read about new topics. They follow their curiosity into deeper understandings of those topics. They snoop around libraries and hang out at field stations. They check out what their enemies have written lately and make plans to outdo their enemies with even smarter essays of their own. They let their minds wander. They come up with all sorts of interesting questions and then poke around looking for information that will help to answer them. By assigning that essay, they've essentially said, "Join me. This is cool."

So join them already. It really *is* cool. Don't write an essay about something you already understand just because it's easy and you can do it. That's not farting around. Don't recycle old work you've turned in for other classes. And for the love of all things academic and good, don't download or buy an essay and pass it off as your own work. When you do any of the above, you don't learn anything worthwhile, and you certainly don't develop an appreciation for what it means to fart around within that discipline. What a waste of tuition! What a waste of time! What a waste of education!

Do you find the assignment boring? That's not the assignment's fault. The assignment knows exactly how much fun it could be if you would just use your imagination and stop worrying about what the professor is looking for. Fart around with that topic! Take a closer look and let yourself wonder about it until you find a question that amuses or intrigues you, a problem that makes you wonder about solutions, an idea you'd really like to test. Then use that same curiosity to dig deeper into the details of that topic. Find a new understanding for yourself.

Don't run away from supposedly boring or difficult topics and beg to write about something you already understand.

College is here to stretch you into something much larger and more interesting than your current self, so you can count on assignments that require you to look at new topics about which you know little or nothing. That's a good thing. That's what you or your parents or *someone* is buying with all that tuition — new topics, new ideas, a new version of you.

Educating yourself can be painful at times, but the fun and satisfaction really are out there and waiting for you and your imagination. If you rise to that challenge, you'll soon find out that there are no bad topics or boring assignments. This is *your* education, student writer. Get out there. Fart around.

CPSIA information can be obtained at www.ICGtesting.com
Printed in the USA
LVOW12s0949310714

396903LV00001B/2/P